LE PÉRÉGRINATEUR
é d i t e u r

*Despite the care taken in researching this guidebook,
in accordance with French legislation (Toulouse14/01/1887)
the publishers cannot be held responsible for
any unintentional errors or omissions.*

*Whilst every effort has been made to ensure that the information
in this guidebook is correct at the time of going to press,
opening times and prices can change without warning and
shops/restaurants close. The publishers will be happy to receive
your comments and suggestions for future editions.*

This guide is also available
in French under the title:
Le Guide de Toulouse.

© - Le Pérégrinateur éditeur
    5, rue Pharaon - F - 31000 Toulouse.
    Tel: + 05 61 14 05 72 - Fax: + 05 61 32 98 81.
    www.leperegrinateurediteur.com

    Authors: Helen ISAACS & Jeremy KERRISON / TELELINGUA.
    E-mail: info@telelingua.co.uk / www.telelingua.co.uk
    Photography: Pascal PISKIEWICZ
    Director of publication: CATHERINE PISKIEWICZ-MAZÈRES.
    Layout: LE PÉRÉGRINATEUR éditeur.

    6th edition
    Registration of copyright: March 2007.
    ISBN: 2 - 910352 - 46 - 3

The
Practical
GUIDE
to
TOULOUSE

Toulouse, the capital of the Haute-Garonne department and the Midi-Pyrénées region, is situated on the Garonne river, in a plain midway between the Mediterranean sea and the Atlantic ocean, surrounded by well-cultivated agricultural land which produces cereal crops, maize and sunflowers.

The city is southern in feel and climate - winters are mild and summers hot - but tends to be compared more often with either Florence or Barcelona than the southern French towns of Provence: the red brick of the city turns our thoughts to Italy, while the vibrant atmosphere of the hot summer nights is distinctly Spanish. The city is both large and small: the population of 760,000 makes this the fourth largest metropolitan area in France (after Paris, Marseilles and Lyons), and yet the old centre can be crossed on foot in twenty minutes. Its lively, cosmopolitan atmosphere is also due in part to the presence of some 140,000 students; Toulouse boasts the second largest university population after Paris, while the

city's international outlook is further enhanced by its twin city links with Atlanta (USA), Bologna (Italy), Tel Aviv (Israel), Tchongqing (China), Elche (Spain) and Kiev (Ukraine).

Natives of Toulouse claim that their city enjoys the perfect location: it is just a two-hour drive to the Pyrenees mountains for skiing in the winter and also about two hours along the motorway to the Mediterranean beaches in the summer. Toulouse can be one of the hottest places in France in July and August with temperatures reaching 35°C (95°F) and its narrow, medieval streets provide welcome shade from the glare of the sun. Spring tends to be the rainiest time of year, winters are generally mild, while autumn, often the most beautiful season, can provide warm days right up to Christmas. Just as Provence has its *mistral* wind, so Toulouse is blown by the *vent d'autan*, a dry, usually warm wind from the south. On clear days the Pyrenees can be seen from Toulouse, a bad omen which locals say guarantees rain within forty-eight hours.

*The first
formal
meeting
of the
Jeux
Floraux,
3 May 1324.
Painting by
Jean-Paul
Laurens
(1912).
Capitole.*

LANGUAGE AND CULTURE

During the Middle Ages, France was divided
linguistically into two halves: the northern part of
the country spoke *langue d'oil*, and the southern
part *langue d'oc* (*oil* and *oc* meaning "yes" in the
respective languages). The inhabitants of Toulouse
spoke what is known as *Occitan*, or the *langue
d'oc*, a language which has a number of different
dialects, among them Gascon and Provençal, and
the court of the county of Toulouse was the centre
of a flourishing literary culture. At this period,
Occitan was above all the language of the
troubadours. Poets who wandered from court to
court, entertaining with their songs and poems,
the troubadours often wrote of "courtly love",
and produced lyrics dedicated to various ladies
of the courts.

In 1323, seven nobles who aimed to
maintain the Occitan language set up what was
initially called the *Compagnie du Gai Sçavoir*,
the oldest of all literary societies in Europe. Each
year, on the 3rd May, the best poets were awarded
flowers. In 1694, this festival became known as the
Académie des Jeux Floraux or Floral Games. The
tradition still exists today and writers who have
been honoured in this way include Ronsard and
Victor Hugo.

The annexation of the south to the Kingdom
of France was however eventually fatal to the
Occitan language, and in the 16C French became
the only official language of the land. Occitan
began quietly to die out until a renewal of interest
was brought about by the publication of some
original troubadour poetry at the beginning of
the 19C.

Nowadays the *Escola Occitana*, founded in 1919, and the *Institut d'Etudes Occitanes de Toulouse*, founded in 1945, aim to promote the language and arrive at a standardised Occitan understood by all speakers of the language.

HISTORICAL OUTLINE

The first recorded inhabitants of the Toulouse area are thought to have been the Volques-Tectosages, a Celtic tribe who settled on the banks of the Garonne in the 3C BC.

A century later much of southern France was colonised by the Romans. Toulouse was situated at the western-most point of the province of *Gallia Narbonensis*; records of the time refer to the city as Tolosa. The wealth of the colony, which had a population of about 20,000, derived mainly from the importing of wine and the trading of local products such as wheat and cheese, or marble from the Pyrenees. Nowadays fragments of the 3km 1C city wall can be seen in front of the Tourist Office, in the *Rectorat* car park in Place Saint-Jacques, and in the Place du Parlement. Remains of a Roman Theatre have been discovered by the Pont Neuf and the site of the *Capitolium*, or temple, was uncovered in 1992 during work on the metro in Place Esquirol. The only monument from this period open to the public is the Roman amphi-theatre at Purpan, just outside the centre of the city.

Gold Gaulish torques (necklaces) dating from the 2C BC, found in Fenouillet (Haute-Garonne), in the region inhabited by the Volques-Tectosages tribe. Musée St-Raymond.

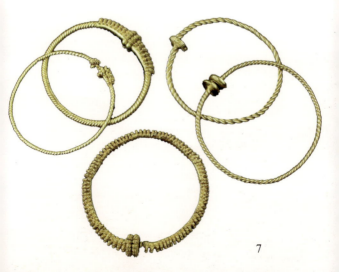

7

Antiquity also survives in the layout of the old town; the *cardo maximus* or main north/south road can be traced along the Rues Pharaon, Filatiers, and St-Rome, from Place du Salin to Place du Capitole, while a fine collection of Gallo-Roman artefacts from the area can be found in the Musée Saint Raymond. The first mention of Christianity in the history of Toulouse comes with the martyrdom of St Sernin (in French) or Saturnin (in Latin), the first bishop of the city. The legend recounts how Sernin, refusing to deny his faith and worship pagan gods, was attacked by a furious crowd about to sacrifice a bull outside the temple. The martyr was attached to the half-crazed bull, and dragged down the temple steps and out of the town, to the street now known as the Rue du Taur (*taur* = bull). His remains were buried secretly by the Christian community on the site of the present Eglise du Taur, and later moved to a shrine at the present Basilica of St Sernin.

Bust of Emperor Augustus, Chiragan. Late 1C BC/early 1C AD.

By the 3C much of the Roman Empire was under threat. The city's defences were reinforced by erecting a rampart along the river, the remains of which are visible at the Institut Catholique. The Visigoths conquered the area in 418 and until 507 Toulouse was the capital of a kingdom which stretched from the Loire to the Straits of Gibraltar. Subsequent invaders included the Franks, Moors and Normans and in the 8C it was Charlemagne who created the County of Toulouse. Originally this was part of the Kingdom of Aquitaine which belonged to the French monarchy,

but gradually the power of the Counts increased until they controlled a vast territory in which the Oc language was spoken. In the 11C and 12C this extended from the Garonne to the Pyrenees in the south, to the Dordogne in the north and as far as the Rhône river to the east.

Sigillary stone of Alaric II, king of the Visigoths. Sapphire and solid gold. 484-507.

As a result of his frequent absences from Toulouse, in 1189 the Count granted certain powers to the municipal councillors, known as *capitouls*, who wielded legal, judicial, financial and military power. On being elected *capitoul* a town councillor had the right to a coat of arms, to a noble title, and could build a tower on his house (some of which remain today). Any power he had was, however, limited, as each *capitoul* was elected for a period of only one year.

The annexation of the county of Toulouse to the kingdom of France was brought about by a chain of events which started with the development of a Christian "sect" in the 12C. Today we refer to these breakaway Christians as Cathars (the word is thought to come from the Greek *katharos*, meaning pure) or Albigensians. In the Middle Ages, they were considered heretics by the Roman Catholic church for having rejected the authority of the Pope and the sacraments of the established church; the Cathars themselves, however, referred to their priests as "*parfaits*" (perfects) or "*bons chrétiens*" (good Christians). Their beliefs spread quickly in the south-west, causing alarm in the established church; events reached a head when the Papal Legate was murdered in St-Gilles in 1208. The Count of Toulouse was suspected of having a hand in the murder and the Pope reacted by

High altar in the choir of St-Sernin Basilica with altarpiece depicting the martyrdom of Saint Saturnin, sculpted by Marc Arcis in 1720.

excommunicating the count and declaring the only crusade ever to take place on French soil. The Albigensian Crusade was as much a political as a religious conflict and the knights from the north who took part in the crusade were promised not only spiritual but also material rewards.

The most famous crusader was a knight by the name of Simon de Monfort, who succeeded in making major gains in territory in the area around Béziers and Carcassonne, but was finally killed in Toulouse in 1218. A plaque by the entrance to the Jardin des Plantes marks the spot where he met his death, formerly just outside the city walls.

The crusade was brought to an end in 1229, by the Treaty of Paris or Meaux. This treaty united the House of Toulouse to the French monarchy through the marriage of Raymond VII's only daughter, Jeanne, to Alphonse de Poitiers, brother of St Louis, King of France. As part of the treaty the University was founded, in an attempt to counteract heretical beliefs with the teaching of theology and canon law. The effort of the established church to reassert its authority can be seen in the rather forbidding, fortress-like style of the Jacobins church, typical of Southern Gothic architecture. Toulouse, and with it much of the south-west, finally became incorporated into the kingdom of France in 1271, after Jeanne and Alphonse had died leaving no heirs.

It was only after the Hundred Years War (1337-1453) that a period of prosperity began. This was to last for around a century and was mainly due to commerce linked to a plant cultivated in the area roughly corresponding to the triangle formed by the towns of Toulouse, Albi and Carcassonne, a region which was to become known as the *pays de cocagne* or land

Toulouse against Montfort by Jean-Paul Laurens (1890). Capitole, Salle des Illustres.

10

of plenty. The plant, called pastel in French and woad in English, produces a blue dye, which made the fortune of many merchants in Toulouse. These merchants constructed Renaissance-style mansions (*hôtels particuliers*) in the city, and fine *châteaux*, some of which can still be visited today, in the surrounding countryside. At its peak, Toulouse exported this dye to Flanders, England and Italy. Its decline, however, came about rapidly from the 1560s with the discovery of the cheaper indigo from the New World. The 15C also saw the definitive establishment of the *Parlement*, a judiciary and legislative institution, which elevated the status of the town to that of a provincial capital. From the 15C the *Parlement*, situated at Place du Salin, was often to come into conflict with the earlier established *capitouls*.

Capitouls of the year 1535-36, including the woad merchant Jean Cheverry.

After the decline in the woad trade, commerce in Toulouse centred on the production of wheat; in the 17C maize was introduced into the area, and, along with sunflowers and other cereal crops, this is now one of the main crops of the region. The construction of the Canal du Midi, linking Toulouse to the Mediterranean, increased prosperity at the end of 17C. The end of the 18C and beginning of the 19C saw the construction of bridges and the *canal latéral de la Garonne*, as well as the destruction of the cloisters of St-Sernin basilica and St Etienne cathedral. Parts of the town were replaced with new boulevards, in the Parisian Haussman style; the Rue de Metz and Rue d'Alsace-Lorraine,

Pierre-Paul Riquet.

11

the city's two main axes, date from this period. Toulouse had entered a period of decline by the end of the 18C, with the suppression of the Parlement in 1790. The *département* of the Haute-Garonne was created in the same year, and from this moment Toulouse became simply the county town of the *département*. By the beginning of the Second Empire, in 1852, the population had increased to 100,000 but the Industrial Revolution had made little impression on the city. What had been a glittering cultural capital in the Middle Ages and a prosperous commercial centre during the Golden Age of pastel, now became little more than a provincial backwater.

MODERN TOULOUSE
It was only after the First World War that the town came to life once more; in under a century Toulouse has grown from a small, provincial town to one of the most active business and high-tech centres in France. It is now the fourth largest city in France, has the second largest student population after Paris, and boasts a modern, international

The new A380 plane first took to the skies on 24 April 2005.

airport handling an ever-increasing number of flights within Europe and beyond. Its first metro line, opened in 1993 and extended in 2003, will soon be joined by a second underground line running north-south through the city. Toulouse is also linked by train and TGV high-speed rail services to Paris and other European cities.

Pierre-Georges Latécoère.

This startling transformation is largely due to the aviation and space industries. Because of its location away from the battlefields of the First World War, Toulouse became a centre for the manufacture of explosives, cartridges and arms. Pierre-Georges Latécoère, a native of the region, moved his aircraft factory from Lille in the north of the country, where it was threatened by the war, to Toulouse, resulting in the development of the city into a pioneer centre of aviation.

Famous pilots such as Mermoz and Saint-Exupéry flew the first airmails to Morocco, and then to West Africa and South America from the city. This first aircraft factory evolved into Aerospatiale, one of the main players in the

development of Concorde. 1970 saw the birth of Airbus Industrie, Europe's leading aircraft manufacturer. Between 2001 and 2006, Airbus was jointly owned by EADS (80%) and BAE Systems (20%) ; in October 2006, EADS took over 100% ownership of the compagny. Over the past four decades, Toulouse has been involved in the development of a complete family of Airbus (A300, A310, A318, A319, A320, A321; A330, A340 and A380). The launch of the twin-deck A380, and the development of the new wide-bodied A350 have added further strength to Airbus' position in the aviation market. Different aircraft sections are manufactured by Airbus' European partners around Europe, then transported to Toulouse and Hamburg for final assembly (visits to the assembly site are possible - *see p. 54 for details)*. The Franco-Italian ATR passenger plane is also assembled in the city.

The aviation industry is an essential part of the Toulouse economy, but is by no means the only high-tech industry located here. The city has become Europe's leading space centre with CNES (National Centre for Space Research), Astrium, Alcatel Espace and Spot Image, among others, all with their headquarters around Toulouse, while large companies in associated sectors such as electronics (Siemens Automotive, Freescale semi-conducteurs) and software (Thales Avionics) have also migrated to this part of the country.

The administrative headquarters of the Galileo European Satellite Navigation System,

The Galileo satellite project, a joint European Union and European Space Agency initiative, is based in Toulouse.

a joint initiative of the European Commission and the European Space Agency (ESA), are also based in Toulouse. In the academic field Toulouse can boast a number of prestigious universities, over a dozen *Grandes Ecoles*, including SUPAERO, ENAC and ENSICA, which train pilots, aircraft engineers and constructors and air traffic controllers, and numerous research and development laboratories; the city is also the headquarters of France Météo (*French Meteorological Office*).

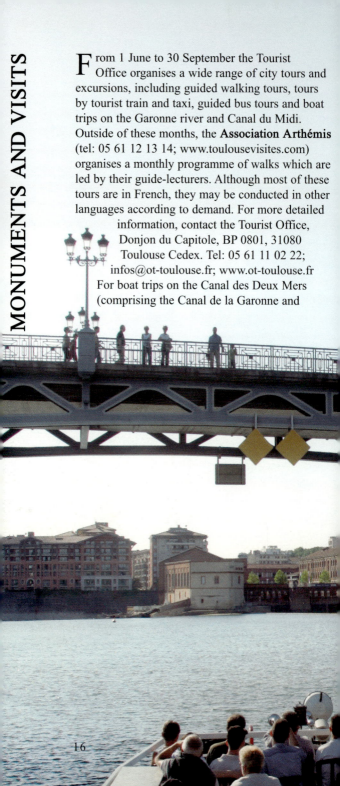

From 1 June to 30 September the Tourist Office organises a wide range of city tours and excursions, including guided walking tours, tours by tourist train and taxi, guided bus tours and boat trips on the Garonne river and Canal du Midi. Outside of these months, the **Association Arthémis** (tel: 05 61 12 13 14; www.toulousevisites.com) organises a monthly programme of walks which are led by their guide-lecturers. Although most of these tours are in French, they may be conducted in other languages according to demand. For more detailed information, contact the Tourist Office, Donjon du Capitole, BP 0801, 31080 Toulouse Cedex. Tel: 05 61 11 02 22; infos@ot-toulouse.fr; www.ot-toulouse.fr For boat trips on the Canal des Deux Mers (comprising the Canal de la Garonne and

the Canal du Midi, which links the Atlantic to the Mediterranean), contact **Voies Navigables de France (VNF)**, the organisation responsible for the rivers and canals of southern France (**Direction Interrégionale Sud Ouest**, tel: 05 61 36 24 24; www.vnf.fr). Detailed information leaflets on cycling along the canal towpaths are available from **Association Vélo** (5, avenue François Cillognon, 31200 Toulouse; tel: 05 34 30 94 18). Bicycles can be hired at Square Charles de Gaulle, opposite the Tourist Office, from **Movimento**, Monday-Friday, 8am-7pm and weekends 10am-7pm; costs: 1€ for a half-day, 2€ for a full day, and 3€ for 24 hours (5, port St- Sauveur, 31000; tel: 05 34 300 300; www.movimento.coop).

Toulouse
Plan de l'hypercentre

0   100   200   300m

GEOSIGNAL
CARTOGRAPHIE

Rapas

Réalisation : GEOSIGNAL - Toulouse - 05 61 21 00 01
www.geosignal.fr

MUSEUMS

There are a number of interesting museums in Toulouse, some private and others owned by the municipality. For visitors spending some time in Toulouse, a museum pass, valid for a month, is available at a cost of €6 for three museums or €9 for six. These passes are valid for the following museums: Les Abattoirs, Musée des Augustins, Musée Paul Dupuy, Musée Georges Labit, the cloisters of the Jacobins church, the Fondation Bemberg and Musée Saint-Raymond.

N.B.: Most museums are closed all day Tuesday.

Museum d'Histoire Naturelle

Jardin des Plantes

35, allées Jules-Guesde. Tel. 05 62 22 21 86; www.museum.toulouse.fr
Bus stop: Jardin des Plantes.

Dating back to the early 19C, Toulouse's Natural History museum is closed for restoration at the time of going to press (*scheduled to open in 2007*). An ambitious project is underway to modernise the museum, renovating the current building and adding a new glass section and mezzanine level, making this one of the largest museums of its kind in Europe. Standing in the attractive 19C botanical gardens of the Jardin des Plantes, the museum will focus on mankind's relationship with nature and the environment through its collection of more than 700,000 exhibits.

Molar tooth of a mammoth, discovered in Toulouse.

Musée St-Raymond

Place St-Sernin. Tel: 05 61 22 31 44. Bus stop: Concorde.
Annexe at 28, rue Salenques open for sales of postcards and books.
Open daily, 1 June - to 31 August, 10a.m. -7p.m.;
1 September to 31 May, 10a.m. - 6p.m.
€3; no charge on the first Sunday of the month.

This museum houses exhibits dating from the Bronze Age to the year 1000, including an exceptional collection of antique sculptures. The display on the second floor (*Tolosa en Narbonnaise*) is dedicated to Toulouse during the Roman era and includes a number of lapidary pieces and rare exhibits, such as statues of emperors from Béziers and Gallic gold necklaces from Fenouillet. The first floor presents a selection of antique items from the Villa de Chiragan, not far from Toulouse, including reliefs of the Labours of Hercules and a group of portraits of emperors and private individuals. The basement of the museum houses remains of the palaeo-Christian necropolis of Saint-Sernin, as well as a number of sculpted sarcophagi.

The Abduction of Proserpine, marble low relief dating from the Roman period. Villa de Chiragan.

Musée des Augustins

21, rue de Metz - Tel: 05 61 22 21 82; www.augustins.org.
Metro stop: Esquirol - Bus stop: Augustins.
Open daily, 1 June - 30 September: 10a.m - 6p.m. and Wednesdays
until 9p.m.; otherwise 10a.m. to 5p.m. and Wednesdays until 9p.m.
€3; no charge for children under 18, students or on the first Sunday of the
month. Guided visits of the museum take place daily in French. Closed Tuesdays
and public holidays. Organ concerts are held at 8p.m. on Wednesdays.

This municipal fine arts museum is housed in a former Augustinian monastery begun in 1309. The monastery's religious community was disbanded at the time of the Revolution and the building has been used as a museum since the end of the last century. The museum is best known for its outstanding collection of Romanesque sculpture, taken from the cloisters and chapterhouses of Toulouse destroyed during the last century.

On entering the museum the visitor is led immediately into the cloisters which display a collection of sarcophagi, gargoyles and keystones. From here doors lead off to various rooms: the salle capitulaire or chapterhouse houses a collection of mainly Gothic tombstones and sculptures, including the famous 15C Nostre Dame de Grasse, a sculpture from the Toulouse school, depicting the young Virgin and child. In the church a number of religious paintings can be admired, including a work by Rubens (Christ and the Two Thieves). Temporary exhibitions are occasionally held in the church.

Nostre Dame de Grasse (second half of the 15C). Polychrome sculpture.

The museum's justly famous collection of Romanesque sculpture, including one of the most important collections of Romanesque capitals in the world, is housed in a light and airy room just off the cloisters. Over half of the capitals come from the monastery of Notre-Dame de la Daurade, the oldest of which date from around 1100-1110 and show similarities with the cloister capitals at Moissac; the rest are from the cloisters of St-Sernin and St-Etienne. In an adjacent gallery a series of engraved medieval inscriptions is exhibited. The first

Oarsmen adorning a late-12C capital from Notre-Dame de la Daurade church.

floor of the museum is dedicated to painting, and exhibits works ranging from the 17C to the 19C. Artists include Delacroix, Ingres and Toulouse-Lautrec, as well as painters from Toulouse such as Tournier and Chalette. The monumental staircase leading up to the galleries displays 19C plaster cast statues. In the summer, classical concerts are held in the cloisters - contact the Tourist Office or the museum for a detailed programme.

Musée Paul Dupuy

13, rue de la Pleau. Tel: 05 61 14 65 50. Bus stop: Carmes.
Open 1 June to 30 September, 10a.m. - 6p.m.;
1 October to 31 May, otherwise 10a.m. - 5p.m. Closed Tuesdays
and public holidays. €3; no charge on the first Sunday of the month.

This museum, housed in a 17C mansion, was established in the first half of the 20C to exhibit the collections of Paul Dupuy, the wealthy owner of a Toulouse department store. It is particularly rich in decorative art - earthenware, an exceptional clock collection, glass, ivory, a collection of musical instruments - and has a 17C apothecary. Coins, drawings, and engravings are also exhibited. Temporary exhibitions are shown on the second floor and are changed approximately every three months.

11C horn known as the "Horn of Roland", part of the Saint-Sernin treasury.

Musée du Vieux Toulouse

7, rue du May. Tel: 05 61 13 97 24.
Metro stop: Esquirol. Privately owned. Open 15 May to 15 October, 2-6pm.
Closed Sunday and public holidays. Guided tours in French on Wednesdays and Fridays at 3pm. €2.20. Closed in 2007.

The museum is housed on the first floor of the Hôtel du May, built in 1590 for Antoine Dumay, the physician of Queen Marguerite of Navarre.
It presents collections relating to the history of the town, including old maps, paintings, regional art and ceramics. The building has a beautiful tower which is occasionally open and which offers an attractive view over the rooftops of Toulouse.

Musée Georges Labit

17, rue du Japon. Tel: 05 61 14 65 50.
Bus stop: Demouilles. Open 1 June to 30 September, 10am-6 pm;
1 October to 31 May, 10am-5pm. Closed Tuesdays and public holidays.
€3; no charge on the first Sunday of the month.

This museum houses the collections of George Labit, a 19C native of Toulouse attracted to the Far East. A great traveller, he brought back to his home town photographs, stamps, weapons, porcelain and ivory. His impressive collection was donated by his father to the city of Toulouse after his death, along with the neo-Moorish villa which now houses the collection. Since then, the collection has been enriched with other artefacts from India, China, Tibet and other Eastern countries.

Fragment of a jamb (pillar) from a temple door. Uttar Pradesh. 6-8C.

Les Abattoirs

ESPACE D'ART MODERNE ET CONTEMPORAIN
DE TOULOUSE/MIDI-PYRÉNÉES

76, allées Charles-de-Fitte. Tel: 05 34 51 10 60 or 05 62 48 58 00;
www.lesabattoirs.org. Metro stop: Saint-Cyprien.
Open 11am-7pm. Closed Mondays.
€6.10; no charge the first Sunday of the month.

The masterpiece of the museum of modern and contemporary art is Picasso's magnificent stage curtain *La dépouille du Minotaure en costume d'Arlequin* (The Minotaur's Body dressed in Harlequin's Costume) painted in 1936. The collection exhibits more than 2,000 works and offers an overview of artistic trends from the United States, Europe and the Far East since the Second World War.

Galerie Municipale du Château d'Eau

Place Laganne. Tel: 05 61 77 09 40; www.galeriechateaudeau.org.
Bus stop: Cours Dillon.
Open 1-7 p.m. Closed Mondays. €2.50.

This red-brick water tower was built in 1823 and is situated not far from the Pont Neuf in the St-Cyprien district. Abandoned for over a century, it was restored at the initiative of the photographer Jean Dieuzaide and has been used to house photographic exhibitions since 1974. The exhibitions are shown displayed on the two floors of the water tower, and in a small annexe behind the tower. Exhibitions are temporary and change every month.

As a city with an important medieval history, Toulouse has a number of religious architectural gems which should not be missed, the most interesting of which are listed below. *Out of season, most of the churches close between 12 noon and 2pm.*

Basilique St-Sernin

Place St-Sernin. Metro stop: Capitole. Open July to September, Monday to Saturday 8.30am-6.15pm, Sunday 8.30am-7.30pm; June, Monday to Saturday, 8.30am-12.15pm and 2-6.15pm, Sunday 8.30am-12.15pm and 2-7pm; October to May, Monday to Saturday, 8.30-11.45am and 2-5.45pm, Sunday 8.30am-12.30pm and 2-7pm. No charge. **Crypt and ambulatory**: open July to September, Monday to Saturday, 10am-6pm, Sunday 11.30am-6pm; October to June, Monday to Saturday, 10-11.30am and 2.30-5pm, Sunday 2.30-5pm. €3.

The first church on this site was built by Bishop Exupère around the year 400 to house the body of the martyred St Sernin, which, according to legend, was moved from a modest wooden oratory on what is now Rue du Taur.

A monastery, first mentioned in 844, was built to guard the tomb. This building remained until the 11C, when the number of pilgrims visiting the church on the way to Santiago de Compostela was so great that a bigger building was required. The present church was started around 1080, and was consecrated by Pope Urban II on 24 May 1096. Construction was carried out in a number of stages and the church was finally completed in the 14C.

The church is built of brick and stone, in the form of a Latin cross with double aisles flanking the nave and radiating chapels around the apse and on the east side of the transepts. In the 19C, restoration work was started by the architect Viollet-le-Duc, who made some alterations to the building itself (these alterations were reversed during the restoration work of the 1990s) and opened up the area around the church by destroying the monastery buildings, such as the cloisters. Outside the church it is worth admiring the view of the five semi-circular radiating chapels in contrasting colours of brick and stone from the end of Rue St-Bernard, with the octagonal structure of the belfry towering above them. Heading clockwise around the church, you will come to the three portals of the church, the first of which is the **Porte des Comtes**, constructed from 1082-83 and dedicated to St-Sernin. To the left of the doorway are the three sarcophagi which give the doorway its name: these originally held the tombs of the family of the Counts of Toulouse. **Porte Miègeville**, further west, was decorated around 1115. The tympanum develops the theme

Console on Porte Miègeville depicting King David.

of the Ascension in which Christ is depicted being lifted to heaven by angels. Standing in front of the doorway is a Renaissance archway, formerly part of the 16C enclosing walls. The upper triangle section of the arch dates from 19C and was added by Viollet-le-Duc.

Sculpted reliefs from the main entrance to the church, the **west portal** (1115-1118), have been moved to the Musée des Augustins. Above this portal eight capitals are carved with delicate representations of plants, animals and human figures. The interior of the church is typical of the great pilgrimage churches. The side aisles allowed pilgrims visiting the church to make their way to the ambulatory and the chapels displaying relics, without interrupting the services taking place in the nave.

The quality of the sculpture in the church is remarkable, with numerous carved capitals of various designs dating from the late 11C and early 12C. The majority are sculpted with floral and vegetal carvings, while others depict religious scenes. Many of these capitals are in the tribunes, and as a result are rather difficult to see without binoculars. The tour of St Sernin led by the Association Arthémis (*in French*) often includes access to the galleries, from where the capitals can be better admired.

Also remarkable for its carving is the famous 11C **altar table**, which can be seen through the 18C choir enclosure. The altar is marble and thought to have been of pagan origin, possibly used for sacrifice. It is finely sculpted on the sides

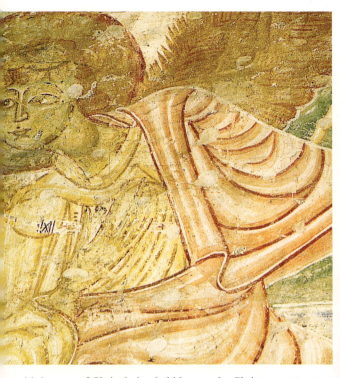

with images of Christ being held by angels, Christ and the Virgin Mary, the apostles, and a frieze of birds facing each other and is signed by the stone-carver, Bernard Gilduin. St Sernin is buried beneath the 18C Baroque baldaquin behind the altar. In the 1970s plaster and paint applied in the 19C were removed and the alternating brick and stone revealed, as well as several medieval wall paintings. It is probable that all the apsidal chapels were once painted with frescoes. The largest of those remaining is in the north transept; on the west wall, it tells the story of the Resurrection and dates from around 1180.

There is a charge to visit the **apse** and **crypt** (*see above*). Here can be seen the five radiating chapels where pilgrims of old processed to venerate the various relics of saints.

The basilica had some 178 different relics, many of which were supposedly given to the church by Charlemagne. On the inner wall of the ambulatory are seven late-11C marble reliefs.

The Angel of the Resurrection - detail from the Romanesque fresco depicting the Resurrection of Christ (west aisle of the north arm of the transept).

29

The figure of Christ, surrounded by the symbols of the four Evangelists, is thought to be by Bernard Gilduin, the sculptor of the altar, as are the carvings of the seraph and cherub on either side of Christ. Most of the wooden, gilded shrines in the chapels belong to the Counter-Reformation period; these were removed during the restoration work by Viollet-le-Duc and stored in the tribunes. They were replaced by imitation Gothic shrines, one of which is still in place. In 1980, the 17C shrines were restored and replaced in the chapels, and it is now the turn of the imitation Gothic shrines to be kept in the tribunes. It is also possible to visit the upper crypt, which was ribvaulted in 1258 when the relics of St Sernin were removed from the crypt and placed under a heavy canopy in the church, and the lower crypt, vaulted in the 14C. A number of reliquaries can be seen, but many, including the most valuable, have been transferred to the Musée Paul Dupuy. The abbey buildings which surrounded the church were destroyed in the early 19C; these included the great Romanesque cloister (several of the cloister's magnificent capitals are preserved in the Musée des Augustins), the chapter house, the abbot's dwelling and canonical buildings. A car park now stands in their place where a flea market is held every Sunday.

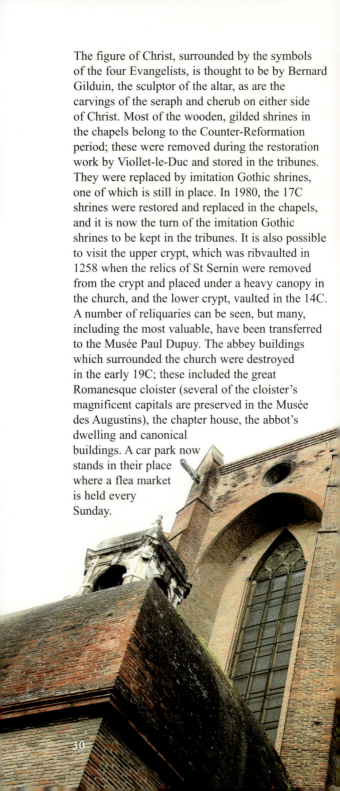

Eglise des Jacobins

Rue Lakanal. Tel: 05 61 22 23 82. Metro stop: Capitole.
Open daily from 10am-7pm. Cloisters:
€3; no charge the first Sunday of the month.

The Dominican order was founded in Toulouse by Domingo de Guzman from Castile - later to become St Dominic - in 1215. De Guzman had stopped in the region on his way to Spain from Italy in 1206 and was horrified by the Albigensian heresy which he found flourishing here. His small community was initially lodged in buildings donated by Pierre Seilan, a wealthy Toulousain, not far from the Château Narbonnais. Later, the monks moved into larger buildings in Rue St-Rome and then in 1229 work began on a church and monastic buildings on land situated near the old Roman wall between the city and the bourg. By 1230 the Dominicans had arrived in Paris, settling close to Porte St-Jacques, hence the name Jacobins. Construction of the church and monastery - which included the first university in Toulouse - started in 1230 and the church was consecrated in 1234.

31

Only the doorway of the Western façade remains of this first Romanesque building and research has shown that four different building campaigns took place between 1230 to 1335. After the Revolution, the Jacobins church was requisitioned by the Artillery, and was badly damaged. The building has survived thanks to the writer Prosper Merimée, who initiated a lengthy programme of restoration in the 19C. The church is a masterpiece of Southern Gothic, a style which has little in common with the flying buttresses of the Ile-de-France Gothic churches in the north. Southern Gothic reflected both the spirit of poverty of the first Dominicans, and the proselytising role of the church, so fundamental to the Catholic church after the Albigensian crusades and the Cathar heresy. Entering the church, you will perhaps be surprised by its unusual layout. Instead of the more usual central nave and side aisles, here the church is divided into two bays of roughly equal width: the south received the public and the north the clergy.

Entering the church, the visitor is struck by the boldness of the 7 columns which spread into ribs comparable to the leaves of a palm tree.

Detail from the paintings in Chapelle St-Antonin.

Having been completed around 1340, the church was chosen in 1369 by Pope Urban V of Avignon as the final resting place of St Thomas Aquinas, who had died in Fosanova, Italy, in 1274. The relics of the saint lie in a 19C gilded wooden casket beneath the main altar of simple marble. 80m long, 20m wide, and with columns reaching 22m in height, the Jacobins is among the highest churches in the Gothic architectural style. One of the columns, slightly wider than the others, supports 22 ribs, which radiate from it to the vault like the leaves of a palm tree. There is an entrance fee for the remains of the monastery buildings, which include all of the eastern wing: the chapter house, the Chapelle St-Antonin, the refectory (which has been restored and holds art exhibitions) and the cloisters. In the summer, evening concerts are held in the cloisters - contact the Tourist Office for details.

Cathédrale St-Etienne

Place St-Etienne. Metro stop: Esquirol.
Bus stop: St-Etienne.
Open July to September 10am-7pm; October to June 10am-noon and 2-7pm.

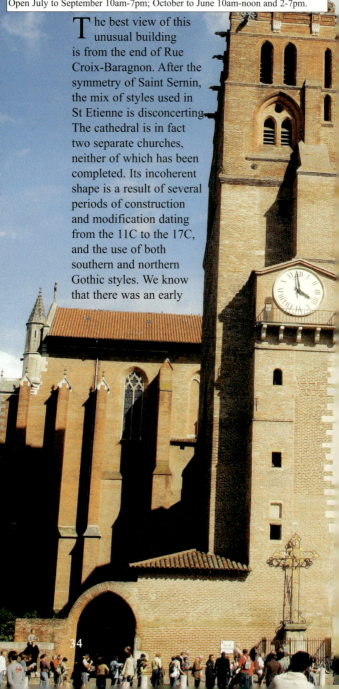

The best view of this unusual building is from the end of Rue Croix-Baragnon. After the symmetry of Saint Sernin, the mix of styles used in St Etienne is disconcerting. The cathedral is in fact two separate churches, neither of which has been completed. Its incoherent shape is a result of several periods of construction and modification dating from the 11C to the 17C, and the use of both southern and northern Gothic styles. We know that there was an early

Christian church on this site around the 4-5C, close to the 1C Gallo-Roman wall, although no trace of this building remains. The first mention of the cathedral is in a charter which dates from 844 and which mentions the three existing churches of Toulouse of that time - St-Etienne, St-Sernin and the Daurade.

However, it was in the 11C that Bishop Isarn, having found a ruined and deserted church on this site, undertook to rebuild the edifice. Vestiges of his Romanesque building, such as some finely carved capitals, can be seen on the walls of the current nave. Work on this church finished around 1140 with the construction of cloisters and other monastic buildings to the south of it. The cathedral was transformed at the beginning of the 13C. Its vast nave - 19 metres wide - was built according to the principles of the developing southern Gothic style, which called for a large nave and no side aisles. As was the case with St-Sernin, construction was interrupted in 1211, during the Albigensian crusade. The nave was hastily vaulted and construction brought to a halt. At the end of the 13C, Bishop Bertrand de l'Isle undertook the construction of a new cathedral. He demolished the Romanesque chancel and rebuilt it in northern Gothic style. The great arcs, the ambulatory, the chapels and high windows all date from this period; the church was completed up to the triforium and then covered with a wooden roof. As a result of both the death of the bishop in 1286 and loss of financing, a new nave was never built, and so the earlier nave remains, perturbingly out of line with Bertrand de l'Isle's chancel.

After the fire of 1609 which destroyed the wooden roof of the apse, it was decided to place the present vaults on the entire structure.

The finely-carved walnut choir stalls also date from the 17C.

Inside the cathedral the beautiful stained glass windows date from the 14C, 15C and 20C. The modern window in the nave portrays the main figures in the history of the building. The 16C and 17C tapestries which hang in the nave and the choir stalls were made in Toulouse; those in the nave depict the life of various bishops of the city (Sernin, Exupère, Hilaire) and those in the stalls the life of St Stephen (Etienne in French).

Saint Christopher, stained glass window (15C).

The elaborate 17C altarpiece shows the martyrdom of St Stephen, surrounded by statues of the Evangelists. From the gardens - Square Cardinal Saliège - the visitor has a good view of the fortress-like bell-tower and the side of the cathedral which was completed as recently as 1937. The north portal is a copy of the flamboyant Gothic south portal. Houses once existed in this spot, but these were destroyed in the 19C. The sign for the Rue des Cloches, which used to run alongside the cathedral, can be seen on the cathedral wall.

The cathedral cloisters and other buildings were destroyed between 1812 and 1817, when Rue Sainte-Anne was extended. Judging from the remains exhibited in the Musée des Augustins, the capitals dated from the 12C.

Chapelle des Carmélites

1, rue du Périgord. Tel: 05 61 21 27 60.
Bus stop: Jeanne d'Arc Bayard.
Open June to September daily, except Mondays, 9.30am-1pm and 2-6pm;
October to May, daily except Mondays, 10am-1pm and 2-5pm.

Beautifully decorated with Baroque paintings by Jean-Pierre Rivalz and Jean-Baptiste Despax, this single-nave 17C chapel is all that remains of the Carmelite convent.

Eglise St-Pierre-des-Chartreux

23, rue Valade. Bus stop: Arsenal.

This early 17C church was built by the Carthusian monks of Saix, near Castres, after they were forced to flee their monastery during the Wars of Religion. For two centuries it was decorated by artists from Toulouse and as a result now houses one of the best collections of classical paintings in the city.

37

Eglise
Notre-Dame-de-la-Daurade

Place de la Daurade. Bus stop: Pont-Neuf.

The origins of the church are unclear, although it is thought that there was already a church on this site in the 5C. The church became a Benedictine priory in the 11C and a cloister was built. Named for the gold mosaics which decorated it, the old church was destroyed in 1759 for safety reasons. The present building dates from the end of the 18C and was consecrated in 1838. Inside the rather gloomy interior of the church can be seen an early 19C Black Madonna and child, a copy of the 14C wood statue burned in 1799. The priory cloister was pulled down in 1811, though fortunately some of the splendid 11C capitals were saved and now form a major part of the magnificent collection exhibited in the Musée des Augustins.

Eglise Notre-Dame-de-la-Dalbade

Place de la Dalbade. Bus stop: Carmes.

This church, the fourth on the site, was built between the end of the 15C and the middle of the 16C. Its red-brick façade contains a flamboyant rose window and its tympanum is decorated with a colourful 19C ceramic copy of Fra Angelico's *Coronation of the Virgin* by Gaston Virebent.

Eglise St-Pierre-des-Cuisines

Place St Pierre. Bus stop: Arsenal. Tel: 05 61 22 31 44.
Open Mondays 10am-1pm; guided tour (in French) at 11am. Also open daily
31 July to 31 August, 10am-noon and 2-7pm; guided tour (in French) at 4pm.

This medieval church was once a priory and was badly damaged at the end of the 18C. A portal with 12C Romanesque capitals and a medieval tomb in a recess in the wall which once marked the border of the cemetery can, how ever, still be admired. The church now houses an auditorium and a dance school.

There are approximately 30 *hotels particuliers* or town mansions in Toulouse: the 16C hôtels concentrated in the commercial area around the Rue St-Rome and the later 17C and 18C hôtels, built by the parliamentarians, in the area around St Etienne. The existence of these fine buildings is largely due to two factors. Firstly, the fire of 1463 destroyed over 8,000 houses and so after this date much rebuilding was needed; secondly, this date corresponded with the beginning of Toulouse's Golden Age, during which the cultivation and exploitation of woad brought great wealth to the city and allowed rebuilding in the new Renaissance style to take place. Most of these hôtels are still privately owned and so cannot be visited. The visitor can, however, often enter the first courtyard and admire the external decoration.

Hôtel d'Assézat/Bemberg

Rue de Metz. Tel: 05 61 12 06 89; www.fondation-bemberg.fr
Metro stop: Esquirol. Bus stop: Pont Neuf. Fondation Bemberg:
open 10am-12.30pm and 1.30-6pm (9pm Thursday). Closed Mondays.

Self-portrait on a white background by Pierre Bonnard (c. 1933).

One of the great Toulouse *hôtels*, the Hôtel d'Assézat has undergone an extensive restoration programme and can now be seen in all its Renaissance glory. Built for the woad merchant, Pierre d'Assézat, in the mid-16C, it was designed by Nicolas Bachelier, the most important architect working in the region at that time. In its simple, homogenous style and carefully balanced sense of proportion the hôtel is typically Renaissance. The columns framing the windows in the north wing reduce in size towards the top of the building and are placed in the ancient order of Doric, Ionic and Corinthian. Italian influence is felt in the open loggia to the south, which dates from the later phase of construction which took place after 1562. A number of changes had taken place between the two phases, notably the beginning of the Wars of Religion and the collapse of the woad market, as a result of the discovery of cheaper indigo. Pierre d'Assézat was a Protestant and therefore directly affected by the Wars of Religion. In 1562 his goods were confiscated and he was exiled from Toulouse for 10 years. He was then pardoned by the King and returned to the city to carry on the construction of his house. However, the architect had since died and d'Assézat had less money so the project was changed and the architect's son took over work.

The fourth wing of the building is simply a wall; there was not enough land left to create a proper wing. It is decorated with flowers, leaves and masks in white stone and has a simple open gallery. The building was privately owned until the beginning of this century when it was left to the city, on the condition that one of the rooms was dedicated to the *Académie des Jeux Floraux*. Nowadays the building houses the collection of paintings belonging to the Fondation Bemberg, which is open to the public.

Elegant door knocker at the Hôtel d'Assézat.

42

Hôtel de Bernuy

Rue Gambetta. Metro stop: Capitole.

This *hôtel* was built by Jean de Bernuy, a Castilian who arrived in Toulouse at the end of the 15C and quickly made his fortune in woad, soon becoming the richest man in the area: it was he who guaranteed the ransom payment for François I when the king was taken prisoner by Charles V of Spain. In thanks, the king paid a visit to Toulouse in 1533 and stayed with Jean de Bernuy.

The oldest parts of the building, the façade and the second courtyard, all date from 1504 and still have some Gothic features, such as the

Jean de Bernuy.

gargoyles around the tower, the pointed windows and the flamboyant Gothic decoration around the doorway. Note the octagonal tower and small circular tower attached to it. This tower was both functional and symbolic: it held a spiral staircase which allowed access to the different rooms off the staircase, the very top room being used as a strong room for valuables. The tower is, however, too high for the building as a whole, a privilege of the capitouls, as a symbol of their power.

The first courtyard dates from a second period of construction; started in 1530 and carried out by the architect Louis Privat, it was built in stone, a sign of great wealth in Toulouse. Two wings remain - a decorative gallery facing the street and the northern wing. Here the decoration is pure early Renaissance, influenced by Italy or the Loire châteaux. In the middle of the northern wing is the coat of arms of the Jesuits.

After the death of Jean de Bernuy, the *hôtel* became a Jesuit college and is still an educational establishment today, housing part of the Lycée Fermat high school.

The first courtyard (1530), the work of Louis Privat, is a pure expression of the Toulouse Renaissance style.

44

Hôtel du Vieux Raisin

This mid-16C Renaissance hôtel was built for a lawyer, Menier, and is unfortunately in need of restoration. The most impressive windows are those to the left on entering the courtyard which depict three stages of life: old age, maturity and childhood. It is also worth crossing the courtyard to admire the spiral stone staircase in the tower.

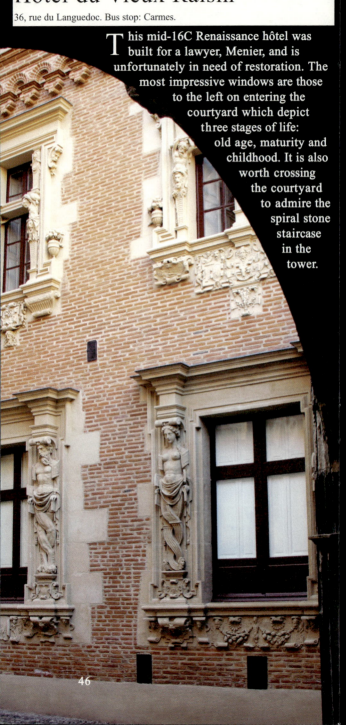

Hôtel des Chevaliers de St-Jean-de Jérusalem

32, rue de la Dalbade. Bus stop: Carmes.

I t is thought that the Knights of St John took up residence here around the beginning of the 12C. The present building, the work of Jean-Pierre Rivalz, was commissioned by the knights to replace the earlier Romanesque construction. It dates from the 17C and was supposedly inspired by the Chigi palace in Rome.

Hôtel de Clary
also known as Hôtel de Pierre

25, rue de la Dalbade. Bus stop: Carmes.

B uilt in 1538 for Jean de Bagis by the famous architect Bachelier, this *hôtel* is the most famous in the street. Antique marbles were added to the building at the beginning of the 17C by François de Clary, along with the rather heavy façade. A particular feature of Bachelier's work are the powerful Atlantes which support the pediment of the west doorway.

HIC THEMIS DAT JVRA CIVIBVS
APOLLO FLORES CAMOENIS
MINERVA PALMAS ARTIBVS.

The Capitole

Place du Capitole Tel: 05 61 22 29 22.
Metro stop: Capitole. Open during office hours and on Saturdays.

A long with St Sernin, the Capitole building is one of the most familiar of the Toulouse sights. The name Capitole has evolved from Chapter - Capitulum in Latin and Capitol in Occitan - and has nothing to do with the Roman Capitolium or temple which was situated in Place Esquirol. The Capitole is the seat of the municipal authorities and has been so for over eight centuries. In the 12C the Count of Toulouse had direct or indirect rule over a vast territory, and so town councillors or capitouls gradually assumed a range of powers during the Count's absences. The buildings of the capitouls at this time covered much of what is now Square Charles de Gaulle.

The fire of 1463, which started south of the city and burnt for 10-12 days, destroyed over 8,000 houses, and also damaged the Capitole buildings. Nothing remains of these original buildings and nowadays the oldest part of what was once the Capitole is the building referred to as the Donjon situated in Square Charles de Gaulle. The word "donjon" actually means keep, although in this case the tower has never been part of a castle. The architecture is military in style, with crenelations and machicolations, and small towers on each corner, and Renaissance in period, although only the windows are actually Renaissance in style. The building was originally the Tour des Archives; all municipal records were kept on its first floor and the tower came to be a symbol of the power of the capitouls. The slate roof was added in the 19C by Viollet le Duc; originally the roof would have been tiled. Nowadays, the Tourist Office is situated in the Donjon.

The present Capitole building is a mix of styles dating from the 16C to 19C; the side facing the Donjon is relatively recent and dates from 1884. It is the façade, however, which is the best-known part of the Capitole.

Cour Henri-IV on a wedding day.

This magnificent neo-Classical structure is the work of Guillaume Cammas and dates from 1750-60. Cammas's work is particularly remarkable in that it gives a homogeneous look to the building, while the buildings behind the façade are not at all homogeneous.To visit the Capitole, enter either from Place du Capitole or from Square de Gaulle. The Place du Capitole entrance leads you into **Cour Henri IV**. This courtyard dates back to the beginning of the 17C and boasts a fine Renaissance gateway begun by Nicholas Bachelier in 1546. Above the arch is a statue of Henri IV. Note also the arms of the city of Toulouse, which show the Château Narbonnais (no longer extant but formerly situated near the present Place du Parlement), St-Sernin basilica, the Occitan cross carried by the Agnus Dei and the French *fleur de lys*. The execution of Henri de Montmorency, Governor of Languedoc, on 30 October 1632, following an uprising against Richelieu, is commemorated by a marble plaque in the floor. The galleries in the courtyard date from 1602-1605 and show many of the coats-of-arms of the *capitouls*.

Entry to the rooms of the Capitole building is through a door by the Square Charles de Gaulle entrance. A plaque on the wall opposite the door commemorates the granting of powers to the *capitouls* by the Count of Toulouse in 1189. Inside, the entrance hall is decorated with fine 19C paintings by artists from Toulouse, such as Jean-Paul Laurens. The bust in the entrance hall is of Jean Jaurès, a native of nearby Castres in the *département* of the Tarn, who was a town councillor in Toulouse.

Three galleries can be visited on the first floor of the Capitole. The first is the old **Salle des Mariages**, no longer used for weddings. The 19C paintings in this room are by Paul Gervais and have the theme of love as their subject. The second gallery is the **Salle Henri Martin**, with two long murals by this painter in Impressionist style: one depicts country scenes painted at different seasons of the year, while the other is a city-scape with the banks of the Garonne as its subject. All the people

Salle des Illustres, an anthology of 19C Toulouse Art.

in the painting actually existed and have been identified; the most famous is Jean Jaurès, the bearded figure sporting a beige coloured raincoat and a boater, with his hands behind his back. The third room is the **Salle des Illustres**. The present room was inaugurated in 1897 and is similar to the 17C Salle des Illustres, only a little bigger. This is a gallery in Italian style: a long room, with many windows, mirrors, paintings and marble columns. Much of what we see, although magnificent, is imitation: the paintings are not frescoes, and the columns are not made of marble (some of the "marble" columns are even signed, and have been adorned with insects and butterflies). The room is decorated by the work of about 10 different artists, including a large painting by Benjamin Constant representing the arrival of Pope Urban II in Toulouse at the end of the 11C, and a remarkably detailed composition by Jean-Paul Laurens which depicts the people of Toulouse building the ramparts of the city at the time of the Albigensian crusade. This large room is currently used for civil marriages, and as the two sets of chairs show, on busy days two weddings occasionally take place at the same time.

This large painting by Benjamin Constant represents the arrival of Pope Urban II in Toulouse at the end of the 11C.

Canal du Midi

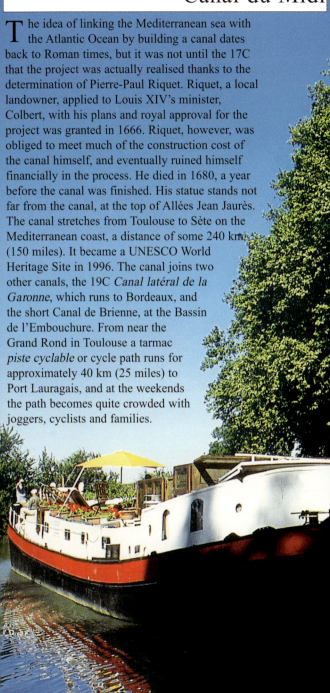

The idea of linking the Mediterranean sea with the Atlantic Ocean by building a canal dates back to Roman times, but it was not until the 17C that the project was actually realised thanks to the determination of Pierre-Paul Riquet. Riquet, a local landowner, applied to Louis XIV's minister, Colbert, with his plans and royal approval for the project was granted in 1666. Riquet, however, was obliged to meet much of the construction cost of the canal himself, and eventually ruined himself financially in the process. He died in 1680, a year before the canal was finished. His statue stands not far from the canal, at the top of Allées Jean Jaurès. The canal stretches from Toulouse to Sète on the Mediterranean coast, a distance of some 240 km (150 miles). It became a UNESCO World Heritage Site in 1996. The canal joins two other canals, the 19C *Canal latéral de la Garonne*, which runs to Bordeaux, and the short Canal de Brienne, at the Bassin de l'Embouchure. From near the Grand Rond in Toulouse a tarmac *piste cyclable* or cycle path runs for approximately 40 km (25 miles) to Port Lauragais, and at the weekends the path becomes quite crowded with joggers, cyclists and families.

Airbus tours

Three tours are available, all run by the Taxiway company (www.taxiway.fr).
Tours should be booked well in advance by calling + 33 (0)5 34 39 42 00
or by e-mailing reservation@taxiway.fr. A valid passport or identity card
is required for all tours.

The first, the Jean-Luc Lagardère tour (1 hour), focuses on the construction of the Airbus A380, providing visitors with an introduction to the A380 programme, a general tour of the construction area, as well as an opportunity to view the assembly hall of this spectacular twin-deck aircraft and its testing stations from purpose-built sightseeing platforms. Cost: €14.00 (adult); €11.00 (children aged 7-18); free for children aged 6 and under.

The Clément Ader tour (1 hour) concentrates on the Airbus A330/A340/A340-500/600 fleet, including an external tour of the assembly site followed by a visit inside the Clément Ader assembly hall to view construction of the A330, A340 and A340-500/600 aircraft at close quarters. This tour also offers an opportunity of a close-up of the extraordinary A300-600 ST Beluga transporter plane. Cost: €9.50 (adult); €8.00 (children aged 7-18); free for children aged 6 and under.

The Concorde tour, which is only available as an add-on in conjunction with an A380 or A330/A340/ A340-500/600 visit, provides a comprehensive introduction to this famous aircraft, including an visit inside the plane. Cost: €4.50 (adult); €3.00 (children aged 7-18); free for children aged 6 and under.

Cité de l'Espace

Avenue Jean Gonord.
On leaving the city centre take the road to Castres. Before the ring-road (*rocade*), follow signs to the Parc de la Plaine and head for the space rocket.
If approaching from the ring-road, take exit 17.
Bus n°37 from Jolimont metro station.
Tel: 0 820 377 223 or 05 62 71 64 80; www.cite-espace.com.
Open 1 July to 30 August and weekends, public holidays and during school holidays 9.30am-7pm; 1 September to 30 June weekends 9.30am-6pm, weekdays 9.30am-5pm. Closed Mondays (apart from July and August).

The city's Space Museum is located on a 3.5 hectare site alongside the ring road, to the east of Toulouse. The museum is divided into three sections. Outside, in the park, visitors can admire a 55-metre model of the Ariane 5 rocket, and other exhibits giving information on the planets and solar system, while inside, three floors of presentations introduce a range of space-related subjects using simulations, experiments and interactive exhibitions.

The Mir space station can also be visited at the museum. Facilities inside the building include a 140-seat planetarium, a gift shop and a café.

The largest park in Toulouse is situated not far from the cathedral and the *Quartier des Antiquaires*, along the Allées Jules Guesde. Known as "les jardins", this park is in fact three separate gardens - the **Jardin Royal**, the **Grand Rond** and the **Jardin des Plantes** - linked by a couple of footbridges, which allow the visitor to stroll from one garden to the next without being forced to negotiate the heavy traffic along the boulevards. The Jardin des Plantes was laid out in 1730 by the Scientific Society for the teaching of botany. Towards the middle of the 18C it had an excellent reputation, surpassed in variety only by the Jardin du Roi in Paris. All three gardens have attractive flower beds and the Jardin Royal and Jardin des Plantes also have a pond each, with ducks and

swans. There is a café in the Grand Rond, as well as in the Jardin des Plantes. The Jardin des Plantes, or Botanical Gardens, is the largest of the three gardens; it provides a number of amusements for children, such as bike hire and various rides, and is also home to the Museum d'Histoire Naturelle. The other large park in Toulouse is situated the other side of town on Boulevard Lascrosses. This is the **Jardins Compans-Caffarelli**, also attractively landscaped with beautiful flowerbeds, paths and a pond in the popular Japanese Garden. The **Prairie des Filtres** provides a pleasant green area for a stroll along the west bank of the river, on the St-Cyprien side of town, while gardens have also been created in the University area behind St-Pierre-des-Chartreux church, on Rue Valade.

Practising football skills around the Grand-Rond fountain.

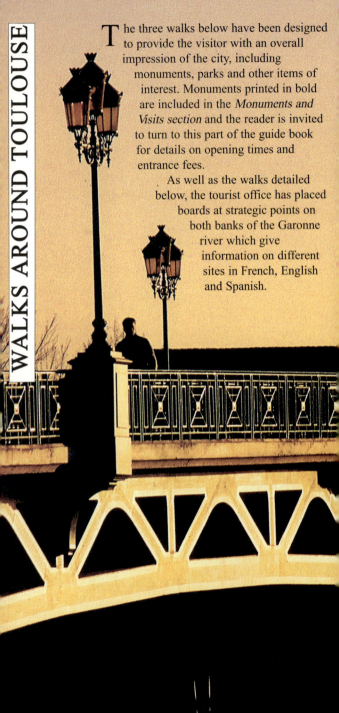

The three walks below have been designed to provide the visitor with an overall impression of the city, including monuments, parks and other items of interest. Monuments printed in bold are included in the *Monuments and Visits section* and the reader is invited to turn to this part of the guide book for details on opening times and entrance fees.

As well as the walks detailed below, the tourist office has placed boards at strategic points on both banks of the Garonne river which give information on different sites in French, English and Spanish.

The bell-tower of St-Nicolas church behind the Pont St-Pierre at sunset.

THE CAPITOLE BUILDING, ST SERNIN, THE BANKS OF THE GARONNE
AND THE JACOBINS CHURCH.

Time: 1/2 day (including visits)

*This walk introduces the visitor to the largest existing Romanesque church
in Europe, and the magnificent southern Gothic Jacobins church, and takes
in some of the lesser known sights of the city. It also includes a stroll along
the banks of the river, a favourite Sunday promenade for Toulousains.*

S tanding in the Place du Capitole, the visitor is in the largest square of the city. The medieval section of the city stretches to the south, while the old medieval *bourg* of St Sernin lies to the north. This square was the limit of the old Roman town and the line of the former *cardo maximus* can still be traced along Rue St Rome, Rue des Filatiers and Rue Pharaon. Cafés and restaurants line three sides of the square. The fourth side is occupied by the magnificent Capitole, the façade of which dates back to the middle of the 18C and which houses the City Hall and the Théâtre de Toulouse. It is possible to visit the public galleries of the Capitole which contain some fine paintings. The square itself was created between 1811-52. It is considered to be the centre of the city and is the focal point for many public events in Toulouse, as well as being used occasionally for open-air concerts. A market takes place here every Tuesday, Wednesday and Saturday with stalls selling fruit and vegetables, organic produce, clothes, bric-a-brac and old books. Beneath the square is a large underground car-park. Note the large bronze Occitan cross on the paving in the centre. It is thought that the cross was chosen in the Middle Ages as the flag of Languedoc, possibly by Raymond IV. It has 12 balls - a symbolic number - which are usually empty; here the artist, Raymond Moretti from Nice, has adapted the cross into a modern design and has chosen to add the 12 signs of the Zodiac in the balls. Moretti is also the artist who created the 29 coffers on the arcades of the square. These paintings attempt

Toiletries given to guests at the Hôtel du Grand Balcon, where the pioneering Aeropostale pilots once stayed.

View from Saint-Exupéry's room in the Hôtel du Grand Balcon, Place du Capitole, on market day.

60

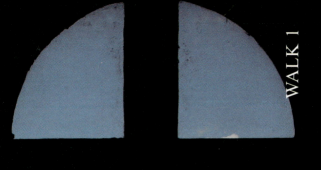

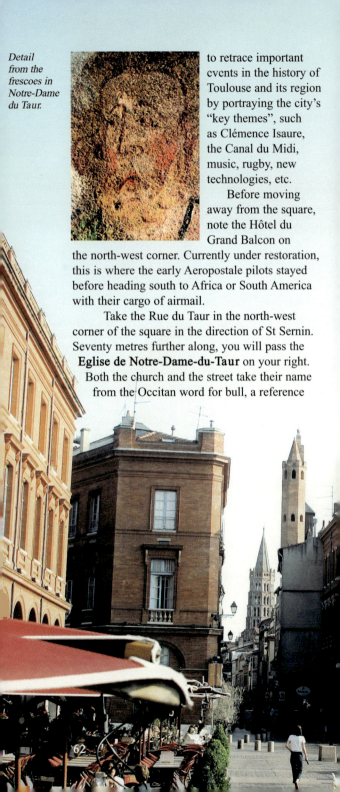

Detail from the frescoes in Notre-Dame du Taur.

to retrace important events in the history of Toulouse and its region by portraying the city's "key themes", such as Clémence Isaure, the Canal du Midi, music, rugby, new technologies, etc.

Before moving away from the square, note the Hôtel du Grand Balcon on the north-west corner. Currently under restoration, this is where the early Aeropostale pilots stayed before heading south to Africa or South America with their cargo of airmail.

Take the Rue du Taur in the north-west corner of the square in the direction of St Sernin. Seventy metres further along, you will pass the **Eglise de Notre-Dame-du-Taur** on your right. Both the church and the street take their name from the Occitan word for bull, a reference to the legend of Saint Sernin, who was supposedly dragged out of town by a half-crazed bull. According to legend, the Eglise du Taur was the first burial place of the remains of the martyred saint; it was known as St-Sernin-du-Taur until the 16C. The church dates from the 14C and

Copy of the seal of the Université de Toulouse.

15C and is built in southern Gothic style. Inside the church, two paintings depict the martyrdom of St Sernin, notably a 19C work above the altar by the artist Bernard Bénézet.

Back on the rue du Taur, stand away from the church to admire its clocher-mur, a flat, wall-like bell-tower, which is very typical of the Toulouse area. Part of the University is situated in this part of town, which explains the number of small cafés and snack bars.

Place du Capitole and the Rue du Taur, which leads to Basilique St-Sernin. Notice the silhouette of Notre-Dame du Taur church on the right.

Sunday morning flea market in Place St-Sernin.

Before coming to the end of the street, note on your left at n° 69 the monumental doorway designed by Bachelier in the middle of the 16C, which now leads to the Cinémathèque de Toulouse (see *Cinema* p. 84) and the entrance to the University library opposite. Turn right into Rue du Périgord to admire the 17C **Chapelle des Carmélites**, a Baroque chapel which is all that remains of the Carmelite convent. The architecture is simple in style and the paintings between the windows are by Jean-Pierre Rivalz and were inspired by the ceiling of the Sistine Chapel.

Retrace your steps to Rue du Taur, and at the end of this street you will come into Place St-Sernin; in front of you is the celebrated **Basilique St-Sernin** (see p. 26), the largest conserved Romanesque church in Europe and an important staging post on the pilgrims' path to Santiago de Compostela. For the best view, stand to the east of the cathedral at the end of Rue St Bernard by Café St-Sernin. On Saturday and Sunday mornings, a large flea market is held in Place St-Sernin. Along Rue St Bernard the ABC cinema often has a good selection of British and American films, shown in English with French subtitles. To continue the walk, head west away from the church, passing the **Musée Saint-Raymond** (see p.21) on your right. This museum houses an important collection of Gallo-Roman relics (statues, jewellery, etc.). Retrace your steps one hundred metres down the Rue du Taur and

then turn into Rue de l'Esquile, the second street on your right. Take the first street on your left, Rue des Pénitents Gris, and then the first on your right, Rue du Collège de Foix. This is the heart of the medieval university area and along this street can be seen the 15C college founded by Cardinal Pierre de Foix, behind a high wall, and opposite it, remnants of the 13-14C Couvent des Cordeliers - a convent from which only the bell-tower and a section of the gateway remain. Continue to the end of Rue du Collège de Foix, turn left into Rue Deville and then right into Rue Pargaminières which leads down to the river, some 300 metres further on. The road leads to Place Saint-Pierre, from where you follow the quai St-Pierre on the right to the Chaussée du Bazacle - the site of a former medieval mill. In 1889 the mill was converted into a hydro-electric plant which, since 1946, has been operated - and continues to be operated - by the French Electricity Generating Board (EDF). Today, part of the building has been converted into a cultural centre, known as the EDF Bazacle, showing a wide range of temporary exhibitions. Take the steps leading from Place St-Pierre to the riverside walkway, the Quai de la Garonne, constructed in the 18C. Across the river is the Saint-Cyprien district, where two large buildings stand out: the domed Hospice de la Grave immediately opposite and the Hôtel-Dieu Saint-Jacques at the end of Pont Neuf, both of which have evolved from hospitals and hospices founded in the Middle Ages. Part of the old 15C covered bridge is attached to the Hôtel-Dieu St-Jacques.

The riverside walk starts close to the Chaussée du Bazacle, the old river ford, and is usually quite busy on sunny Sunday afternoons. Families stroll by the river, mountaineers practise their skills on the steep, red-bricked walls and the lively atmosphere is enhanced by occasional drummers and musicians. Follow the walkway to the left, heading towards the **Pont Neuf**. Like its counterpart in Paris, and despite its name (New Bridge), this is actually the oldest bridge across the Garonne; the appellation came from its being the first bridge in the city not to be constructed in wood. It was started in 1544 and took over half a century to complete. Signs dotted along the walkway give information about the area. Before you reach Pont Neuf take the steps which lead up from a large esplanade to Place de la Daurade, at road level. Here the riverbank was once the site of the gardens of the Benedictine monastery of La Daurade, which were destroyed in 1766-77, to create the wharves and port, a scheme developed by Lomenie de Brienne, Archbishop of Toulouse from 1762-1788. On Place de la Daurade is the **Notre-Dame-de-la Daurade** church (see p.38).

Gazing out at the Pont Neuf from the shaded banks of the River Garonne on a sunny day in September.

Follow the Hôtel des Beaux Arts sign into Rue Jean Suau, which then leads into Rue Gambetta and back towards Place du Capitole. This area has a good choice of restaurants, offering Indian, Italian, Thai or regional cuisine. On your left note the **Hôtel de Bernuy** (see p.44), now part of the Lycée Fermat, a high school. Step inside to admire the fine Renaissance courtyard, which dates from 1530 and is the work of Louis Privat. After the Hôtel de Bernuy, turn into Rue Lakanal to visit the second most important church of Toulouse, the **Eglise des Jacobins** (see p.31).

The second courtyard (1504), with its high hexagonal tower, reflects the architectural style of the 16C.

Retrace your steps back to Rue Gambetta and follow the street back into the Place du Capitole.

Time: 1/2 day (including visits)

This walk takes the visitor through some of the most attractive squares of Toulouse, past the Musée des Augustins and to the city's unusual cathedral. From there, we plunge into the chic section of town, full of antique shops, and into a maze of narrow medieval streets, which provide welcome shade in the heat of the summer. This part of Toulouse has an almost village atmosphere, away from the noise of the boulevards, and many of the fine mansions have courtyards and even gardens, with an occasional tree top visible behind high walls.

S tart at the Place du Capitole. Walk through the Cour Henri IV, the courtyard of the **Capitole** building and past the Donjon, which houses the Tourist Office, into Square Charles de Gaulle. The layout of this attractive garden was modified at the time of the construction of the Toulouse metro (opened 1993) and parts of the old Gallo-Roman wall can be seen in the garden between the Tourist Office and the main post office directly opposite. The most central metro station, Capitole, is situated

The Donjon du Capitole, now home to the city's tourist office.

69

The fountain in Place Wilson is adorned with two important figures: the Languedoc poet Godolin, and his muse, the Garonne river, lying elegantly at his feet.

in these gardens. Note the bust of Jean Jaurès (1859-1914), a native of Castres and famous French politician, who was a town councillor in Toulouse, near the steps to the metro entrance. Cross the street at the traffic lights and take Rue La Fayette towards **Place Wilson**. Lively at weekends and in the summer, Place Wilson has a number of cafés and restaurants, all with outdoor tables. This oval-shaped square is also the cinema heart of Toulouse. In the centre of Place Wilson is a small garden, a favourite meeting place for locals on a summer afternoon. The fountain in the middle dates from the 19C; its statue depicts Pierre Godolin, a famous Occitan poet of the 17C.

Take the Rue St-Antoine du T, lined with smart boutiques and cafés, towards Place St Georges. At the intersection with Rue St Jérome, note the interesting sculptures on the wall of one of the modern buildings to the left, which are copies of various works of art in Toulouse.

Place St Georges is one of the oldest and most attractive of all the squares in Toulouse, and is especially lively during the summer months, with crowds sitting out at the café and restaurant terraces until the early hours of the morning. A small fruit, vegetable and flower market is held here every morning, except Mondays, and in the winter the square is brightened by a charming carrousel. The square has been the market centre of Toulouse for centuries and a meeting place for the people of the city; it was also the spot where offenders were placed in the stocks and where public executions took place. On the east side of the square is the magnificent 18C Hôtel de la Fage, built after a fire destroyed the four houses which formerly occupied this spot. Just in front of the hôtel is one of the three Wallace fountains to be found in Toulouse (in 1872 Sir Richard Wallace gave 100 fountains to the city of Paris; these were quickly copied by other cities) - the other two are found in the Grand Rond and the Jardin des Plantes.

From the square take Rue Boulbonne, which will bring you past a modern fountain graced by a sculpture by the Toulouse artist Labatut (1851-1935), entitled *The River Garonne offering electrical energy to the city of Toulouse*, in an area of the city with a number of attractive

Outdoor cafés and carrousel in Place St-Georges.

courtyards. Bear right past the fountain and then turn left into the semi-pedestrianised Rue des Arts, which leads towards the Rue de Metz.

As you approach Rue de Metz, the Musée des Augustins (see p.22), located in the former Augustinian monastery, is on your right. This fine arts museum boasts a varied collection of exhibits, including paintings, Gothic sculpture and the most important collection of Romanesque sculpture anywhere in the world. The museum building is also delightful, its green cloisters an oasis right in the heart of the city. In front of the museum is a small garden with benches and a fountain.

Cross the busy Rue de Metz, one of the city's main streets opened out between 1867-1884 from the Pont Neuf to the Cathédrale St-Etienne (see p.34) as part of the large urbanisation projects of the time, and continue along Rue des Arts. At the junction of the street with Rue Croix-Baragnon, note the restored half-timbered house on the corner (n° 1), one of the few houses to have survived the fire of 1463. Until the end of the 15C most of the houses in Toulouse were built in this way; wattle/plaster usually covered the wooden beams so that they were not visible.

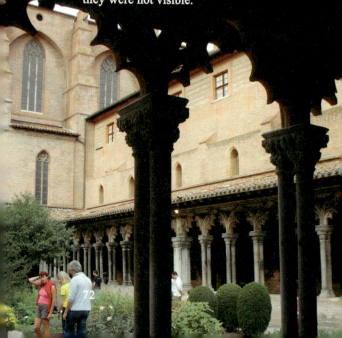

Turning left into Rue Croix-Baragnon, you will notice a number of expensive, chic boutiques. Some of Toulouse's most expensive houses and apartments are found in this part of town. Looking towards the end of the street, you will have the best view of the unusual construction of the Cathédrale St-Etienne. Before heading towards the cathedral, turn right into Rue Croix-Baragnon in order to see one of the oldest houses in the city at n° 15, thought to date from the end of the 13C and known as the Maison Romane. The house has suffered various modifications over the years (notably the top floor extension carried out in 1923 with little respect for the original architecture) but the arched windows, with their animal friezes and finely sculpted capitals, can still be admired.

Retrace your steps to **Place St-Etienne**. The square is now pedestrianised, and an underground car park has been built under the square. As you face the cathedral, the Antique Dealers' District lies to your right, the Préfecture housed in the former bishop's palace of the 17C is situated in the far right hand corner of the square, and the Griffoul fountain is in front of you. This fountain is considered to be the oldest in Toulouse; the obelisk is by Antoine Bachelier and dates from the end of the 16C. The four statues were originally *mannekin pis*, but these were considered improper in the 18C and were replaced by a design considered more appropriate for a religious setting. The square is triangular in shape and is enclosed by a number of fine 17C and 18C houses. To the left of the cathedral is a small garden. A small market selling second-hand books and paintings is held in the square on Saturdays.

Follow the *Quartier des Antiquaires* sign into Rue Fermat which leads into a quiet, select residential area, characterised by narrow streets and private mansions, many of which have fine courtyards or hidden gardens. This is a pleasant area for a wander and the area also has a number of good restaurants and a wide selection of tea rooms.

Rue Fermat opens out into Place Sainte-Scarbes, with its modern fountain. It is worth

heading down Rue Ninau to admire the 16C Hotel
d'Ulmo, and its fine baldaquin over the entrance,
owned by the first President of Parlement, Jean
d'Ulmo. Also near Place Sainte-Scarbes a fragment
of the 1C Gallo-Roman city wall can be seen near
the Rectorat car park in Place St Jacques; in the
same square is the 19C Palais Niel, home to a
Parachute Regiment.

Back in Place Sainte-Scarbes, take Rue
Perchepinte heading away from the cathedral. This
street has a number of well-restored half-timbered
houses. Turn into Rue Espinasse to admire the
magnificent 16C Hôtel de Mansencal, with its mix
of late Gothic and Renaissance features. From

Rue Perchepinte, turn right into Rue Mage, and continue along Rue Bouquières until you reach Rue de Languedoc. Cross the road and follow Rue de la Trinité to the attractive Place de la Trinité, close to Place Esquirol.

From Place Esquirol, the pedestrianised shopping streets of Rue des Changes and Rue St Rome will lead you back to Place du Capitole. Note the different architectural styles of the houses in these streets, from the well-restored half-timbered building topped with a *capitoul* tower on the corner of Rue Peyras, to the 17C Classical style of the Hôtel de Pierre Comère on the corner of Rue Tripière. Two other fine *hôtels* are situated in small streets in this area: Hôtel Boysson at 11, rue Malcousinat, and the 18C Hôtel de Nupces with its magnificent classical courtyard at 15, rue de la Bourse.

The cool, peaceful Place de la Trinité brings to mind a quiet piazza in Rome.

Time: 1/2 day (including visits)

This walk introduces the visitor to one of the oldest parts of Toulouse, south of Place Esquirol. It passes a number of private mansions, starting with the Hôtel d'Assézat, as well as a couple of the city's museums, and includes a stroll through the beautiful public gardens. The walk ends not far from the Musée du Vieux Toulouse which houses a fine collection of paintings, maps and other items and gives the visitor an insight into the history of this ancient city.

Place de la Dalbade, with the doorway of Notre Dame de la Dalbade to the right, and a typical half-timbered house in the background.

The walk starts not far from Place Esquirol, at the **Hôtel d'Assézat** (see p. 40), situated on Rue de Metz, at Place d'Assézat. This, the largest of all the Toulouse *hôtels particuliers*, is now home to the Bemberg Foundation. Its art gallery is open to the public and there are guided tours for visitors in French. The area around Place Esquirol, Place de la Trinité and Place Rouaix was the junction of the two main thoroughfares in Roman times, and it is thought that the location of the Roman forum must have been in this area. During construction work on the car park and metro in Place Esquirol, the steps of the Roman temple were found - roughly at the point in front of the Midica hardware store. From the Hôtel d'Assézat, cross Rue de Metz and

turn right into Rue des Paradoux, heading south away from Place Esquirol. Follow the road until you come to **Eglise de la Dalbade** (see p. 39), the entrance to which is on Rue de la Dalbade. A number of fine, if somewhat neglected, *hôtels* are found in this street. Next to the church, at n° 32, is the **Hôtel des Chevaliers de St Jean** (see p. 47), with, on the opposite side of the road, the famous **Hôtel de Clary** (see p. 47) also known as the **Hôtel de Pierre** at n° 25. The imposing façade of the Hôtel de Pierre dates from the beginning of the 17C; its restored stonework provides a marked contrast with the more usual red brick of the other buildings in the street. The courtyard of the *hôtel* is earlier, dating from 1538, and is the work of Bachelier.

Cross the road from the Hôtel de Pierre and take Rue St Jean towards Place des Carmes. Just before you come to the square, you will pass one of the British-style pubs of Toulouse, the London Town, tucked into a corner on your left. Place des Carmes, formerly the site of the Carmelite

monastery demolished at the beginning of the 19C, is now taken up by a multi-storey car park, the top of which gives a pleasant view of the rooftops of Toulouse. A colourful covered market is held on the ground floor daily, except Mondays.

Walk past the car park until you reach Rue de Languedoc, one of the main intersections created through the medieval town in the last century. Cross the road and turn into the courtyard of 36 rue du Languedoc, the **Hôtel du Vieux Raisin** (see p. 46), a 16C *hôtel* with fine, albeit rather neglected, Renaissance and Baroque decoration. Coming out of the courtyard, turn right and then right again into Rue d'Aussargues, which was intersected by the construction of Rue Ozenne

Monument to Saint-Exupéry by M. Tezenas (2000), Jardin Royal.

during the 19C. A glance at the Gothic parapet and gargoyles on the side of the houses on either side of Rue Ozenne gives an indication of how the street actually destroyed this building in half.

Follow Rue Ozenne away from the centre of town, with the 15C Hôtel de Dahus on your left, towards the public gardens. **Musée Paul Dupuy** (see p. 23) is situated just off this main road to the left, at 11 rue de la Pleau, and has a fine collection of decorative objects. Continue down Rue Ozenne to the entrance of the first of the parks, the **Jardin Royal**, on your left. Bordered on one side by a row of apartment buildings, and on the other by Allées Jules Guesde, this small park, with its picturesque bridge and duck pond, is a favourite setting for wedding photos. A path takes you past the pond, almost to the end of the park, to where an attractive wrought iron footbridge links the park to the **Grand Rond**, also known as the **Boulingrin**. In addition to its colourful flower beds, this park has an old bandstand and a small café for refreshments. A second footbridge links this park with the botanical gardens or **Jardins des Plantes**, the largest of the three gardens, laid out in the 18C. Children are well catered for here, and the park is busy with families on Sundays, with bicycles for hire and pony rides available. There are a number of entrances to this park, which has a large pond, beautiful old trees, a café, as well as ducks, hens, peacocks and various amusements. The **Museum d'Histoire Naturelle** (see p. 20) is also situated in the Jardin des Plantes; it was originally opened in 1865, the museum is currently closed for major restoration and is scheduled to re-open in 2007. To continue the walk, take the exit on Allées Jules Guesde, with the Museum d'Histoire Naturelle on your left. To the left, a plaque commemorates the death of Simon de Monfort, killed near this spot by a missile catapulted from the city walls in 1218 during the Albigensian crusade. Retrace your steps up Rue Ozenne and then turn left into Grande Rue Nazareth, by the small Casino supermarket. This street also has a number of fine town houses and, as always in Toulouse, it is often worth risking a discrete glance into private courtyards.

The façade of the 17C Hôtel de la Belle Paule at n° 16 is particularly attractive. Grande Rue Nazareth runs into Rue du Languedoc, and then into Place du Salin. To your left stand the Law Courts and around the square are a number of half-timbered houses.

Cross the square and turn left into Place du Parlement. A plaque on the wall in this square indicates a small section of the Gallo-Roman wall, as well as the Maison Pierre Seilan, the location of the house where St Dominic lived in 1215. As the name of the square suggests, the old parliament used to be situated in this area, as did the home of the Count of Toulouse, the Château Narbonnais. From here, return to Place du Salin, and take

Dancing on a Sunday afternoon in the Grand-Rond gardens.

the road directly ahead of you, Rue de la Fonderie. At n° 31 is the **Institut Catholique**, which has a small archaeological museum exhibiting Gallo-Roman statuary and part of the 3C Gallo-Roman ramparts. The Institut can be visited as part of a guided tour only.

Turn left into Rue Brunière, and then left again into Rue Pharaon. This road follows the path of the old Roman road and will take you past Place des Carmes, into Rue des Filatiers, Place de la Trinité and up to Place Esquirol. For those interested in learning more about the history of the city, it is worth finishing this walk with a visit to the **Musée du Vieux Toulouse** (see p. 24), situated just off Rue St Rome in Rue du May.

© Patrice NIN

Théâtre du Capitole
www.theatre-du-capitole.org
Orchestre National du Capitole
www.onct.mairie-toulouse.fr
Théâtre de la Cité
www.tnt-cite.com

In addition to its high-tech industries and lively student atmosphere, Toulouse has strong cultural traditions, including a wide range of musical concerts and theatre performances. Overlooking the Place du Capitole, the Théâtre du Capitole hosts ballet and opera, while the excellent acoustics of the Halle aux Grains in Place Dupuy are perfect for classical music. Talented musicians and performers from the Ville Rose include Michel Plasson, once conductor of the renowned Orchestre National du Capitole, and Claude Nougaro, the popular singer who died in 2004 and whose famous song "O Toulouse" is almost a local anthem.

Local theatre was given a boost in 1998, when the newly renovated Théâtre National de Toulouse-Théâtre de la Cité, located just a stone's throw from Place Wilson, was reopened.

During the Bel canto period at the end of the 19th century, the renowned and talented singers of the Capitole gave the theatre a reputation as prestigious as the Liceo in Barcelona or La Scala in Milan. The Toulouse public of the time loved singing and were experts in the art – newcomers to the stage were terrified by the reaction of the audience, who used a range of instruments (whistles, horns, beaters, hammers and reed pipes) to pronounce their verdict on the show.

The Théâtre du Capitole.

83

CINEMA

English-speaking cinema fans are well catered for in Toulouse, with four cinemas all showing films in their original language:

La Cinémathèque: 69, rue du Taur. Tel: 05 62 30 30 11; for information (in French only) on film listings and times, call 05 62 30 30 10 or log onto the centre's website at www.lacinemathequedetoulouse.com

ABC: 13, rue St Bernard. www.abc-toulouse.net

Le Cratère: 95, Grande Rue St-Michel. www.cinemalecratere.com

Utopia: 24, rue Montardy. www.cinemas-utopia.org

The Cinémathèque de Toulouse, founded in the 1950s and housed in the old Collège de l'Exupère, close to St-Sernin Basilica, is a welcome addition to the city's cultural life.

The film collection here is the second largest in France, with films from all over the world, including a notable collection of American burlesque, a Soviet and Russian section, as well as a large number of French films. Facilities here include two cinemas, an exhibition area and a library.

A cinema-concert
at the Toulouse cinémathèque.

© Vincent Lacotte / La Cinémathèque de Toulouse.

85

T oulouse hosts a large number of cultural, art and music festivals throughout the year. These include events dedicated to classical music (*Piano aux Jacobins* in September; *Toulouse les Orgues* in September/October), jazz (*Jazz sur son 31*), world music (*Rio Loco* in June), cinema (*Rencontres Cinémas d'Amérique Latine* in March), fine art, video, sculpture and photography (*Mira* in March/April; *Printemps de Septembre*), dance (in January and February), literature (*Marathon des Mots in June*) and comedy (*Printemps du Rire* in March/April). For further information, log onto the city council's website at www.toulouse-tourisme.com or the Conseil Régional Midi-Pyrénées website at www.festivals.midipyrenees.fr

Piano aux Jacobins, *one of the most atmospheric piano festivals in Europe, has been held in the magical surroundings of the Jacobins cloisters for almost thirty years.*

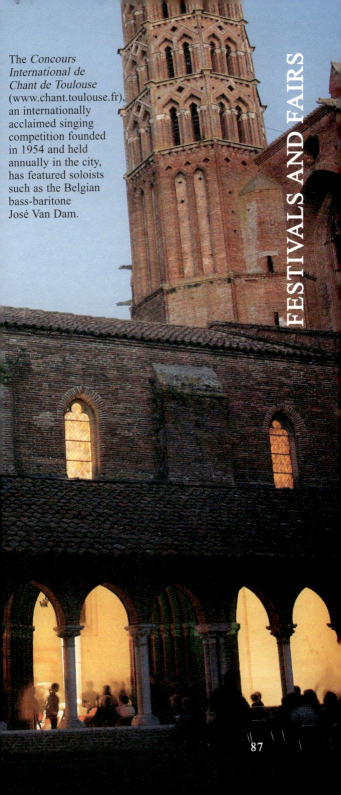

The *Concours International de Chant de Toulouse* (www.chant.toulouse.fr), an internationally acclaimed singing competition founded in 1954 and held annually in the city, has featured soloists such as the Belgian bass-baritone José Van Dam.

FESTIVALS AND FAIRS

Although the city is home to a number of professional teams, it is primarily through rugby union that Toulouse has made its sporting name with famous players from the past such as Jean-Pierre Rives and Jean-Claude Skréla and modern heroes including the likes of Fabien Pelous and Fred Michalak. Its team, **Stade Toulousain**, were French champions on five occasions during the 1990s (their most recent national triumph was in 2001), and were crowned European champions in 1996, 2003 and 2005.

A number of Stade Toulousain players are currently in the French national team, a matter of local pride, and any important win by Le Stade usually brings the crowds out into the streets, waving the traditional black and red colours of the club. The team plays at the Stade des Sept-Deniers, 114, rue des Troënes. For further information on the club, log onto www.stadetoulousain.fr The second major rugby union team in the area is Colomiers, which plays its matches just five miles to the west of the city.

Although Toulouse appears to be dominated by the 15-a-side version, rugby league is also played, while the footballing interests of the city are represented by premier division side **Toulouse Football Club** (www.tfc.info), who play their home matches at Le Stadium, 1 bis, Allées Gabriel Biénès. A wide range of one-off sporting events such as swimming championships, international rugby matches and athletic events are frequently hosted by the city.

The city's racecourse, **Hippodrome La Cépière** (www.hippodrome-toulouse.com), offers a year-round programme for racing enthusiasts, while for those who prefer playing sport rather than watching it, the city has a full range of indoor and outdoor facilities, including swimming pools, skating rinks, tennis centres and some superb golf courses. For skiers, walkers and mountaineers, the Pyrenees are just a couple of hours south of the city. A comprehensive list of all the city's sporting venues and facilities can be found in the *Practicalities section* at the back of the guide.

Local youngsters perpetuating Toulouse's rugby tradition.

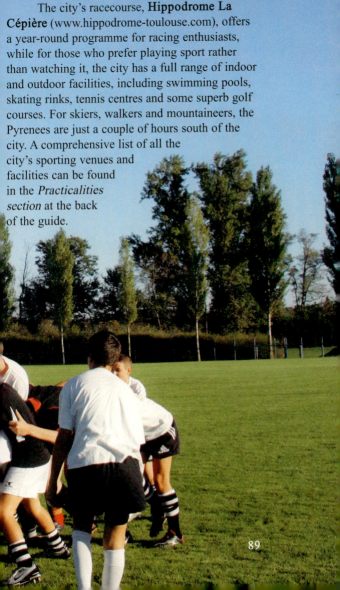

Although the wines produced around Toulouse are yet to establish a widespread international reputation, the region is able to boast two appellations which are growing in popularity both in France and abroad: **Côtes du Frontonnais** and **Gaillac**. They are both among France's oldest vineyards - Frontonnais can date its origins to around the 12C while Gaillac is able to trace its history back to the Gallo-Roman period.

The first can lay claim to being the wine of Toulouse – its vineyards are located on the left bank of the Tarn river and are centred around the small town of Fronton, and the village of Villaudric, 25km (15mi) north of Toulouse. The area, which covers 1,850 hectares, produces both red (75% of total production) and rosé wines (25%), and was designated an Appellation d'Origine Contrôlée (A.O.C.) in 1975; total annual production is approximately 80,000 hectolitres.

The special feature of Frontonnais wines is the use of the unique La Négrette grape – to receive A.O.C. status, wines must contain between 50 and 70% of this grape variety.

The Gaillac vineyards begin about 40km (25mi) northeast of Toulouse and extend over a slightly larger area than those of Frontonnais (2,500 hectares), producing around 120,000 hectolitres annually. Once again, red wine accounts for the majority of production (60%), though Gaillac is reputed for its diversity – its vineyards also produce excellent whites, both dry and sweet, rosés, and sparkling wines, produced according to the *méthode champenoise*. Its whites were granted A.O.C. status in 1936 and its reds and rosés the same privilege in 1970. More recently, the Gaillac vineyards have begun producing *primeur* reds and whites - young wines which are best drunk within 3-4 months of bottling.

| FOOD |

V isitors abroad often wish to sample the local cuisine and eat in authentic restaurants where the menu is usually only in the local language, but find themselves baffled and bemused by a list of frequently incomprehensible choices and reduced to a frustrating method of pot-luck selections.

To help you with your gastronomic discoveries, the *Practicalities section* at the back of the guide includes a concise glossary listing the most common items, both French and regional, that you are likely to encounter in restaurants in Toulouse, while the accompanying list of bars and restaurants - though far from exhaustive - is intended to take the strain out of your gastronomic pursuits. Whether your interest is in sampling local specialities or finding an Italian, Chinese or Indian restaurant, all the information you will need can be found in this section.

© Francis Mauco / Las Crabères

Best value is often at lunchtime, when most restaurants will offer one reasonably priced fixed menu, which may include wine, coffee or both. Some will continue to offer this in the evening, though most will revert to their more expensive menus and *à la carte* dishes; these inexpensive menus are not normally offered at the weekend either. Also look out for daily specials (*le plat du jour*), which will always be part of the fixed menu or can be ordered separately.

A final few words on the somewhat grey area of tipping: if the bill or menu has the words *service compris* included on it, then service is included. You will rarely find a restaurant nowadays which does not automatically include it in its prices, though if service has been good it is customary to leave some small change even if a charge has already been added.

The famous Mulard ducks from the Gers.

93

REGIONAL SPECIALITIES

The gastronomy of Toulouse has much in common with that of neighbouring Gascony to the west and Dordogne and Périgord to the north and places a heavy emphasis on duck and goose products. Visitors unfamiliar with the area and aware only that Toulouse is a southern city may be surprised to find a cuisine which bears little resemblance to the olive oil culture of Mediterranean Provence.

In Toulouse, the traditional dishes tend to be warming winter meals such as *cassoulet*, a heavy bean casserole, or *confit*, various parts of poultry or duck cooked and then conserved in their own fat. The potatoes which are the usual accompaniment to confit are also usually fried in goose or duck fat. Other duck dishes regularly found on the region's menus include *magret* or breast of duck, *gésiers* (gizzards), often served in salads, and, of course, *foie gras* (literally, fatted liver), for which all of southwest France is renowned. Not a calorie-free cuisine by any stretch of the imagination - though medical statistics have shown that levels of heart disease in the Toulouse area are among the lowest in Europe! - but delicious and definitely worth sampling. Probably the best-known dish of Toulouse is *cassoulet*. Not the only place to lay claim to this filling winter dish, Toulouse is challenged by both Castelnaudary and Carcassonne, both of which retain their own versions of *cassoulet*. Tradition maintains that it is Castelnaudary, situated to the southeast of Toulouse on the Canal du Midi which boasts the authentic *cassoulet*, using *fèves* (a type of broad bean) and not dried white beans which were only introduced to France in the 17C. Everyone has their own special *cassoulet* recipe and the secret lies in slow cooking. Ingredients for the recipe include dry beans, garlic, onion speckled with cloves, *bouquet garni*, pork rind, goose fat, confit, Toulouse sausage, even shoulder of lamb or spare ribs, celery, tomato puree and carrots. Most versions will have at least the beans, sausage and a portion of confit.

One product to which the city can safely lay claim is *Saucisse de Toulouse*, a pork-based sausage usually on display in coils and then cut to size. Ideal grilled on its own, it is also an important ingredient of the city's own cassoulet.

For dessert, why not sample one of the region's famed desserts such as the *Fénétra*, an apricot tart, a *Croustade*, a crusty fruit-filled pastry, or a *Pastis Gascon*, an apple-filled pie with filo pastry best sprinkled with Armagnac and warmed in the oven.

Equally *Toulousain* in origins is the crystallised violet (*violette confite*), flowers transformed into sugary sweets, and the *Cachou Lajaunie*, a lozenge taken to help digestion and to freshen the breath which has been produced to the same formula in Toulouse since 1880.

The famous Toulouse sausage.

CASSOULET RECIPE

Serves 4-6 people: 1lb/400g of goose or duck confit. 8oz/200g pork ribs. 5oz /125g streaky bacon. 10oz/250g Toulouse sausage. 4oz/100g goose or duck fat. 1 garlic sausage. 1lb 4oz to 2lb/500g to 800g of dried white beans. 10 garlic cloves. Cooking time: approximately 3 ¹/² hours.

Soak the beans for 4 to 5 hours in cold water, replacing the water regularly. Drain the beans, place them in a large casserole and cover with cold water. Add salt and pepper and bring to the boil over a low heat. Meanwhile, roughly dice the pork and bacon, and peel and chop the garlic.

Fry the diced meat with half of the goose fat for 5 minutes in a large pan. When the beans come to the boil, drain them and then add to the meat in the pan. Cover with cold water

and add the chopped garlic. Season with salt and pepper. Cook for approximately 2 hours over a low heat, stirring occasionally and adding water frequently. Then add the garlic sausage and leave to simmer on a low heat for another hour. After 40 minutes fry the Toulouse sausage in a frying pan with the rest of the goose fat on a low heat. Pre-heat the oven to gas mark 6/7 - 200°C. Once the beans and meat are cooked, pour all the ingredients into a large oven casserole. Add the sausage and goose confit and stir gently.

Place in the oven and cook for 30 minutes, until a fine crust has formed. Serve hot in the casserole dish.

Cassoulet, the local speciality.

The city of Toulouse is at the heart of a relatively undiscovered region full of history, monuments, wonderful scenery and gastronomic pleasures to rival some of France's best-known areas. To help you get the most out of your visit to the region you will find in this part of the guidebook a selection of towns, monuments, museums and other sights which are within easy reach of Toulouse for a day trip or weekend excursion. Approximate distances are given, as are details of public transport (where applicable). Because some of the best sites are off the beaten track, often the best (and only) option to reach them is by car.

Information on tourist offices can be found in the *Practicalities section* on p. 148.

Chateau de Roquefixade, in the Ariège.

Cordes-sur-Ciel is one of the most impressive of the *bastides* (fortified medieval villages and towns) in the region. Founded in 1222 by the Count of Toulouse to re-house the local population badly affected by the Albigensian Crusade, this hill-top town is surprisingly Italian in feel, with examples of Sienese Gothic architecture more usually found in Tuscany than in southwest France. The town is encircled by several ramparts, with impressive fortified gateways that once protected access to the centre. A steep climb leads from Place Jeanne Ramel-Cals, at the bottom of the *bastide*, up narrow medieval streets to Place de la Bride at the top of the town. From here, there are magnificent views of the rolling countryside surrounding Cordes. For visitors wishing to avoid the climb, a "*petit train*" operates in season, running a shuttle service from Place de la Bouteillerie near Place Jeanne Ramel-Cals to Place Fontourniès near the Porte de la Jane (a certain amount of walking is still required to get right to the centre of town!).

The central square is graced by a 14C open-sided market hall, with café tables offering a shady spot for a drink in summer. A deep well in the square dates from the 13C.

The painter Yves Brayer was one of the first artists to settle in Cordes just after the Second World War, prompting a revival of interest in the town and the arrival of other artists and craftsmen. Today the town is home to around thirty studios and workshops, selling original paintings, pottery, leatherwork and clothes.

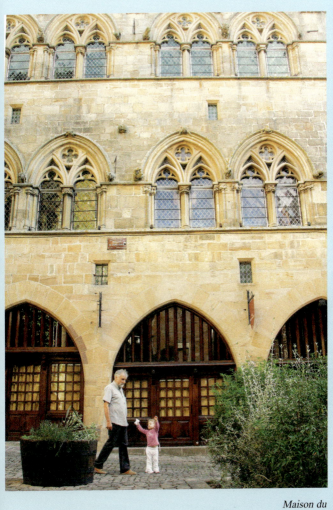

*Maison du
Grand Veneur
(14C).*

La Modiste by Toulouse-Lautrec. Musée Toulouse-Lautrec.

The attractive red-brick town of Albi, built on the banks of the Tarn river in the *département* of the same name, is the birthplace of the artist Toulouse-Lautrec (1864-1901) and home to the Toulouse-Lautrec museum (closed Tuesdays from Oct-March), housing the largest collection of his work worldwide. The museum occupies several floors of the imposing Palais de la Berbie, the old Bishop's Palace, which overlooks Place Sainte-Cécile on one side and the Tarn river on the other. A viewpoint just behind the museum provides excellent views of the river, the museum gardens and the northern district of the town.

Place Sainte-Cécile is dominated by the fortress-like **Cathédrale Sainte-Cécile**. Built in the Southern Gothic style in the 13C and 14C, the cathedral is striking for the contrast between its imposing, austere exterior and highly decorative interior. Of note inside

the cathedral are the ornately sculpted rood screen separating the nave from the chancel and the 15C fresco of the Last Judgement which adorns the western end of the nave. With its compact old centre, Albi is a pleasant town to explore on foot. Its medieval centre consists of a maze of narrow streets (*Vieil Albi*) with attractively restored buildings, including the Hôtel Reynes (now the Chamber of Commerce, but once owned by a wealthy woad merchant), and the half-timbered Maison Enjalbert (now a pharmacy). To the east of the centre, a large square, Place du Vigan, is lined by pleasant terraced cafés and brasseries. A leaflet produced by the Tourist Office details several walks through the town.

The painting of the Last Judgement. This astounding work was produced towards the end of the 15C by an unknown artist.

Sainte-Cécile d'Albi.

S ituated on the banks of the Adour river, in the heart of a fertile agricultural region to the north of the Montagne Noire, **Castres** is an attractive town which comes to life on market days (Tuesday, Thursday and Saturday). The town is also home to a museum of Spanish art, the Goya Museum, which houses three main works and several sketches by the late-18C Spanish artist, plus a selection of works by other Spanish painters (Velasquez, Murillo, Pacheco, Cano, Picasso etc). The museum is located on the first floor of the former Bishop's Palace designed by Mansart in 1675. Opposite the gardens in front of the museum, note the colourful timber merchants' houses with stone cellars opening directly on to the river.

South of Castres, the Montagne Noire separates the Midi-Pyrénées region from the drier landscapes of the Languedoc-Roussillon and the Pyrenees. The mountain range, which extends west to the town of **Revel** (some 50km east of Toulouse), is criss-crossed with footpaths and dotted with lakes.

The colourful banks of the River Agout in Castres.

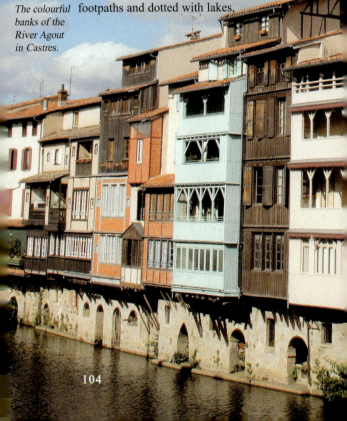

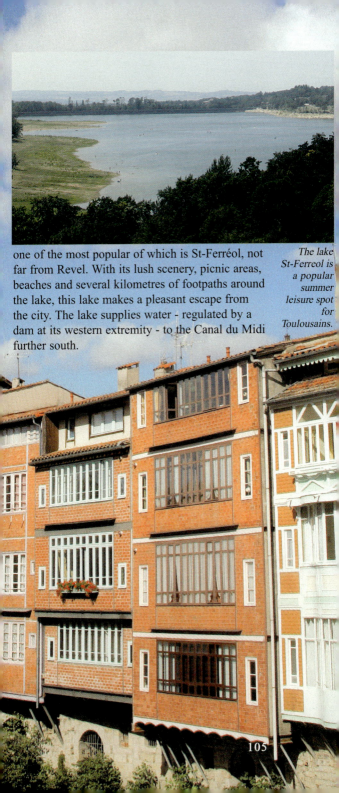

one of the most popular of which is St-Ferréol, not far from Revel. With its lush scenery, picnic areas, beaches and several kilometres of footpaths around the lake, this lake makes a pleasant escape from the city. The lake supplies water - regulated by a dam at its western extremity - to the Canal du Midi further south.

The lake St-Ferreol is a popular summer leisure spot for Toulousains.

© Roumagnac

Head of a
Young Man
*by Ingres.
Musée Ingres.*

An important Protestant town during the Wars of Religion which ravaged the country (and the southwest, in particular) during the late 16C, Montauban is an attractive red-brick town built in typical *bastide* style, with a central arcaded square and grid-like street plan. The town is also the birthplace of the artist Jean-Dominique Ingres (1780-1867), many of whose works can be viewed in the Musée Ingres (closed Mondays from September-June) housed in the old Bishop's Palace overlooking the Tarn river. Situated in the heart of a highly productive fruit-growing area, Montauban is an important agricultural centre with a lively weekly market.

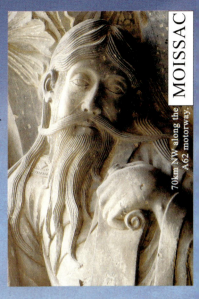

M oissac is justifiably famous for the church and cloisters of the Abbaye de St-Pierre de Moissac, which contain magnificent examples of Romanesque sculpture. The majority of the monastic buildings were originally built in the late 11C and early 12C, including the belfry, cloisters and the original church, although many of the buildings were damaged by fire, the ravages of the Albigensian Crusade, the Hundred Years War and Wars of Religion, and have subsequently been restored or rebuilt. A major campaign to restore the church and cloisters was started during the last century. Particularly remarkable are the tympanum over the church's south entrance and the superb collection of carved capitals in the cloisters. The town lies in attractive countryside on the north bank of the Tarn and is crossed by the *Canal Latéral à la Garonne*.

The prophet Jeremiah depicted on the doorway at Moissac.

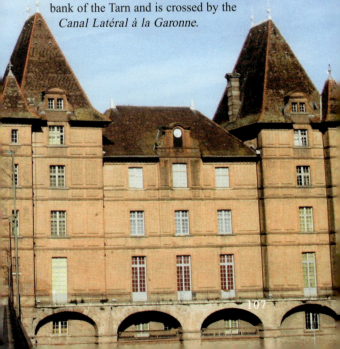

The Aveyron valley is one of the most attractive in France with a number of delightful villages and small towns along its path. **Bruniquel** is well worth a visit, with its picturesque narrow streets, the old Governor's house (Maison Payrol) and two castles (12C and 14C) perched side-by-side above the village and river valley below. Further along the valley, the tiny village of **Penne** hides behind the silhouette of its 13C castle perched on the cliff-top. Also worth a visit is the town

The town hall in St-Antonin Noble-Val is the oldest in France (1125).

of **St-Antonin-Noble-Val**, the main centre for outdoor pursuits in the area (kayaking, canoeing, hang gliding, hiking) and the setting for a colourful local market every Sunday morning. Be sure to drive to the Roc d'Anglars viewpoint overlooking St-Antonin from the high cliff to the south for a

magnificent view of the town and valley. 25km northeast of here is **Najac**, a medieval village built on a ridge above the Aveyron valley, dominated by a 13C castle. A further 20km will bring bring you to **Villefranche-de-Rouergue**, a bastide town which was the capital of the old province of Rouergue. Highlights here include the main square (Place Notre-Dame), overlooked by attractive Renaissance-style buildings and a collegiate church with Flamboyant belfry, and the Baroque Chapelle des Pénitents Noirs (Black Penitents' Chapel). An attractive market is held in the main square on Thursday mornings.

90km NE. Take the A68 to Gaillac, then the D 964 northwest to Braniquel.

AVEYRON VALLEY

Jonah and the whale.
Stained-glass window,
Auch cathedral.

Auch is the heart of the old province of Gascony (the land of the Musketeers) and is now the capital of the Gers department with its gastronomic traditions of duck, goose, foie gras and Armagnac. A fine monumental stairway leads from the Gers river up to the old town, which clusters around the late-15C Cathédrale Sainte-Marie. The cathedral is worth a visit for its richly-decorated choir stalls and its stained glass. The Gers is renowned for its gentle landscapes and relaxed pace of life, and Auch would make a good based from which to explore the area. Sights of interest in the region include the towns of **Fleurance**, **Lectoure** and **Condom**, as well as the charming Romanesque Abbey of **Flaran**, all of which are north of Auch. The bullfighting centre of **Vic-Fezensac** hosts regular bullfights featuring big names from Spain and Portugal, and holds late-night markets during July and August.

The Cistercian abbey at Flaran.

T here are numerous spa resorts in France where "taking the waters" remains a popular way of treating certain complaints and illnesses. The curative powers of the waters in the Midi-Pyrénées region, some of which were already renowned during the Roman period, are many and varied and centres often specialise in the treatment of certains ailments. Spa resorts in the Pyrenees include Ax-les-Thermes, Luchon, Cauterets, Bagnères-de-Bigorre, Aulus-les-Bains and St-Lary-Soulan.

The Pyrenees offer limitless options for outdoor activities throughout the year. The ski season extends from early December to early April,

Learning to ski in the Pyrenees.

with over 50 resorts open to downhill
and cross-country skiers alike on the French
and Spanish sides of the range and in Andorra.
The closest resorts to Toulouse are within just a
couple of hours of the city, making a day's skiing
a feasible option, and include Ax-Bonascre (above
Ax-les-Thermes, south of Foix), Superbagnères,
Peyragudes, St-Lary and La Mongie (all south
of St-Gaudens and Lannemezan to the south-west
of Toulouse).

Outside the ski season the Pyrenees
offer wonderful hiking opportunities through
magnificent and often dramatic scenery.
Options range from relatively easy walking in
the foothills to some seriously challenging hikes
around the higher peaks. Maps and leaflets are
often available from local tourist offices, whereas
detailed maps of footpaths can be purchased in
the bookshops in Toulouse. Other outdoor activities
in the mountains include canoeing and kayaking,
white-water rafting, canyoning and horse-riding.

The town of Foix is dominated by the three towers of its castle.

F oix, the capital of one of France's most sparsely populated departments (Ariège), is the gateway to the Pyrenees, the Cathar castles, Andorra and Spain. The town is dominated by its 13-15C chateau, occupied during Middle Ages by the Counts of Foix, one of whom was the 14C

The ruins of Château de Montségur (Ariège), the last stronghold of the Albigensians. On 28 February 1244, two weeks after the castle was taken, more than 200 Cathars were burnt at the stake for their beliefs.

local hero and warrior, Gaston Fébus. The nearest ski resort, Ax-Bonascre, is located 45km south, with the Andorran border a further 25km away along the N20.

The final stronghold of the Cathars, **Montségur**, lies 30km southeast of Foix. The ruined fortress stands on a rocky outcrop at an altitude of over 1,000m. Here, following the end of the Albigensian Crusade and a long siege (in 1244), 220 Cathars were burnt at the stake, having refused to deny their faith and convert to Roman Catholicism. It is a steep climb up to the ruins, but well worth it for the mystical atmosphere and fine views of the surrounding countryside.

South of Foix, the attractive small town of **Tarascon-sur-Ariège** would make a good base for further exploring the region.

Tucked away in the foothills of the Pyrenees, the village of **Valcabrère** extends over the ancient site of Lugdunum Convenarum, a Roman colony founded in 72 BC. Archaeological excavations have revealed substantial remains of this prosperous town, once inhabited by more than 10,000 people. Also in the village, the Eglise Saint-Just dates from the early Romanesque period and was built using much of the Roman stone from the earlier settlement.Situated above Valcabrère, overlooking the Garonne valley, stands the attractive village of **St-Bertrand-de-Comminges**, an important staging-post for centuries on the route through the Pyrenees south to Spain. With its steep narrow streets and old houses, the town is known mainly for its Cathédrale Sainte-Marie, construction of which began at the beginning of the 12C at the behest of Bishop Bertrand.

Inside the cathedral, the elaborate and imaginative carving of the 16C wooden choir stalls is particularly worthy of note. Also of interest is the carved tympanum over the Romanesque door, depicting the Adoration of the Magi. A music festival, the Festival de Comminges, is held every year in July and August in the village.

Choir stalls in Saint-Bertrand-de-Comminges (detail).

The Romanesque church of St-Just-de-Valcabrère.

117

The town of Carcassonne is divided into two distinct areas: the medieval fortress known as the Cité, situated on a hill on the right bank of the Aude river, and the Bastide Saint-Louis, laid out in the 14C, which stands on the left bank. Built after the Albigensian Crusade, the Saint-Louis district is typical of a bastide town, with its regular grid-style street plan once surrounded by fortifications. However, it is the imposing Cité, one of the best preserved medieval fortresses in Europe, that draws visitors to Carcassonne. With 3km of walls and 52 towers, its origins date back to Gallo-Roman times, although the Cité as it stands today dates mainly from the 12C and 13C. Much of the fortress was restored during the 19C by the architect Viollet-le-Duc, who also worked on Notre-Dame cathedral in Paris and St-Sernin basilica in Toulouse.

Highlights in the Cité include the Basilique St-Nazaire, with its Romanesque nave, Gothic chancel and fine stained-glass windows, and the Count's Castle (Château Comtal), once home to the Viscounts of Béziers and Carcassonne. It was in the dungeon of this castle that Viscount Trencavel was held prisoner after the siege of Carcassonne during the Albigensian Crusade. Guided tours of the château take visitors out onto the inner wall and through some of the towers of the ramparts. The château is also home to a small lapidary museum housing sculptures and sarcophagi from various churches of the region, as well as a comprehensive bookshop.

The summer months are particularly lively in Carcassonne, with a range of concerts and a *Son et Lumière* show taking place in the open-air theatre behind the basilica.

The Cité de Carcassonne was declared a UNESCO World Heritage Site in 1998. A magnificent view of the fortress can be enjoyed from the motorway stop between the Carcassonne Est and Carcassonne Ouest exits.

PRACTICALITIES

Police: Tel: 17 or 05 61 12 77 77.

Main Police Station:
23, boulevard de l'Embouchure.

Fire Brigade: Tel: 18.

Ambulance (SAMU): Tel: 15.

Poisons Unit: Tel: 05 61 77 74 77.

SOS Doctors: Tel: 05 61 33 00 00.

Emergency doctor: Tel: 05 61 49 66 66.

Centre Hospitalier Universitaire de Purpan:
Place du Dr Baylac. Tel: 05 61 77 22 33 (switchboard).

Centre Hospitalier Universitaire de Rangueil:
Avenue Jean Poulhès. Tel: 05 61 32 25 33 (switchboard)

Hôpital des Enfants (Children's Hospital):
For children under 15 years of age.
330, avenue de Grande-Bretagne. Tel: 05 34 55 86 33
(switchboard).

Emergency number: Tel: 05 34 55 84 10.

All-night Chemist:
70 - 76 allées Jean Jaurès (near place Wilson).
Tel: 05 61 62 38 05. Open 8pm-8am.

Emergency Vet: 05 61 50 10 80.

Lost Property: 05 62 27 63 00.

Traffic Information: 05 61 12 77 77.

Arriving in Toulouse

Visitors travelling to the city by air will arrive at the international airport at Blagnac, located about 5km to the northwest of the city. Rail passengers will pull into the main railway station, Gare Matabiau, a 15-minute walk or two stops on the metro system from the heart of the city, while bus passengers will arrive at the new Bus Terminal (*Gare Routière*) just a hundred metres from the train station. Approaching the city by road is a relatively straightforward option; whether you arrive by major road (the A61 from the Mediterranean coast, the A62 from the northwest, the A64 from the south-west, the A20 from the north) or via the numerous minor roads surrounding the city, you will eventually meet the Toulouse ring-road, (*la Rocade*). From here, just follow the signs to Toulouse Centre then consult the map enclosed with this guide.

Airport

Aéroport de Toulouse-Blagnac
Tel: 0825 380 000 (0.15€/min).
www.toulouse.aeroport.fr

The airport is situated approximately fifteen minutes to the northwest of Toulouse. It is an international airport with an increasing number of flights to domestic and international destinations. Current domestic services include numerous daily flights to Paris (both Orly and Roissy-Charles de Gaulle), several flights daily to Nice, Marseille, Lyon, Strasbourg, Nantes and Clermont-Ferrand, plus regular flights to smaller French cities. International travellers can now benefit from several daily flights to London, Madrid, Basle, Munich, Brussels, Milan and Amsterdam, as well as regular scheduled services to Rome, Lisbon, Oporto, Malaga, Basle, Venice, Birmingham, Bristol, Manchester and several North African cities. An increasing number of charter flights also operate in-season to Ile de la Réunion, Guadeloupe, Martinique, Montreal and other popular holiday destinations in Europe and North and West Africa.

Two brochures, the *Guide du Voyageur* (Travellers' Guide) and the *Guide Horaires* (Timetable Guide), both available from the airport information desk, provide comprehensive details on all services and facilities on offer at the airport.

A **shuttle bus** (tel: 05 34 60 64 00; www.navette-via-toulouse.com) operated by *Les Courriers de la Garonne* leaves the airport (Hall B) for the centre of Toulouse every 20 minutes on weekdays and at a reduced frequency at weekends (cost: 4€ single (*un aller simple*); 6€ return (*un aller-retour*) - tickets valid two months), stopping at Compans-Caffarelli, Place Jeanne-d'Arc, the Allées Jean-Jaurès, and the bus station (*Gare Routière*). Journey time is approximately 20 minutes. Reduced rates are available for passengers under 25.

At the airport, tickets can be bought at the shuttle bus desk at the airport or on board. The last departure of this service is at 00.15am. The shuttle service from the city centre to the airport starts at 5am from the bus station and tickets can be bought at the shuttle bus desk at the bus station or on board. The last bus from the *Gare Routière* departs at 8.20pm except Saturday (7.40pm).

Taxis depart from between Halls B and C on the Arrivals level. Approximate fares to/from the city centre are 25€ during the day and €27 at night. Tel: 05 61 30 02 54. In addition, there are a number of car rental companies based at the airport. Their offices are all located in Halls B and C on the Arrivals level.

Airlines

Air Algérie
05 61 30 05 14   www.airalgerie.dz

Air France
3654   www.airfrance.com

Air Lingus
01 70 20 00 72   www.airlingus.com

Alitalia
0820 315 315   www.alitalia.com

British Airways
0825 825 400   www.ba.com

EasyJet
0899 700 041   www.easyjet.com

Fly Be
00 44 1392 268529   www.flybe.com

Iberia
0825 800 965   www.iberia.com

KLM
0890 710 710   www.klm.com

Lufthansa
0826 10 33 34   www.lufthansa.com

PGA Portugalia
0825 083 818   www.flypga.com

Royal Air Maroc
0820 821 821   www.royalairmaroc.com

SN Brussels Airlines
0826 101 818   www.flysn.com

Tunisair
0820 044 044   www.tunisair.com

Airport facilities

An **information desk** (0825 380 000) situated in Hall C on the Arrivals level is open 5.30am-midnight daily (6am-midnight on Sundays) and is able to provide a range of local information including maps of Toulouse and the region, as well as details on hotels and restaurants. Keys, parking tickets etc can be stored at this desk at a cost of 8.50€.

Exchange facilities (Travelex and Banque Populaire) are available on the Arrivals level. Cash machines are available on both the Arrivals and Departures levels.

A **post office** (*La Poste*) in Hall B on the Departures level is open Monday to Friday, 1.15-3pm. Wi-Fi access is also available throughout the airport. Access to the private "*La Croix du Sud*" airport lounge can be pre-booked or arranged directly with the Information Desk on the Arrivals level. Cost: €17.00. A prayer room is available for passengers on the mezzanine level in Hall C (2nd floor).

Taxis

Taxis are plentiful in Toulouse though the habit of hailing one from the street is less of an art form here than in other European cities. As a result, taxi ranks are located strategically throughout the city centre; the ones at Place Wilson, Place Esquirol and Matabiau railway station are available day and night, while those at Place Jeanne d'Arc, Place St-Cyprien and Toulouse Blagnac airport are usually available until early or late evening. If you are not near one of these stands, the following telephone numbers can be called 24 hours a day.

Capitole Taxi	Tel: 05 34 25 02 50.
Taxi Radio Toulousains	Tel: 05 61 42 38 38.

Railway Station

Tel: 08 92 35 35 35. www.sncf.fr; www.voyages-sncf.com
The railway station (*Gare Matabiau*) is situated along Boulevard Pierre-Sémard, about 10 minutes' walk from Place Wilson and the city centre. It is well connected to both bus services and the métro (Marengo-SNCF station) - an underground passageway provides immediate access to the underground system. In addition to its normal ticket desks there is a special information centre which includes an international desk. The station has a reasonable selection of fast-food outlets plus a restaurant serving breakfast, lunch and dinner. The newsagent in the departures area normally stocks a good selection of foreign newspapers and magazines. For visitors arriving in Toulouse, a small Tourist Office is open at the station. There is a huge choice of food and accommodation in the immediate vicinity; cross the Canal du Midi and you are immediately swamped with possibilities - though, in terms of accommodation, the area is not particularly central in relation to the historic part of the Toulouse (*see hotel/restaurant section for recommendations*).

As the largest city in southwest France, Toulouse is well served by the French rail network. The station's main link to the French capital is its three-times daily TGV high-speed run to Paris-Montparnasse (5 hours) via Bordeaux. Alternatively, a regular service still operates between Toulouse and the French capital (6 $^{1/2}$ hours - slightly longer on overnight couchette and sleeper services) via Brive-la-Gaillarde. Regular long-distance trains also run to Marseille, Lyon, Nice, Bordeaux and Nantes. Toulouse also offers a number of international routes, particularly to Italy, with connections via Nice to all major Italian cities. Schedules to Barcelona, Madrid and beyond are slightly less user-friendly and normally require a change of train at either the Mediterranean or Atlantic borders with Spain. On a regional level, touring by train is an easy option with numerous departures to the region's most attractive sites, such as Albi, Carcassonne, Auch and the Dordogne, in addition to the wonderful panoramas of the Pyrenees, and its summer and winter resorts. Train tickets can be bought online, at the railway station or at a number of outlets around the city. In addition, discounts are available for the under-25s, senior citizens, families and passengers booking tickets in advance.

Getting around the city

The best way to see any old town centre is by foot, and Toulouse is no exception. The centre is small enough to allow you to walk from one end to the other in approximately 20 minutes. If your hotel is slightly out of the centre, however, the city has a comprehensive and efficient local transport system, including a modern metro system.

Metro system

The metro (www.tisseo.fr), opened in 1993 and extended in 2003, is clean, comfortable and efficient. To date, the system consists of one line (Ligne A) of 18 stations from Balma-Gramont to Basso-Cambo; construction of a second line (Ligne B), running north to south through the city, is scheduled for completion in two stages during the course of 2007. There is a metro stop at the railway station (Marengo-SNCF) which makes the system handy for anyone arriving in Toulouse by train, and the line goes through the centre of the city, with stops at Jean Jaurès (for Place Wilson and the Boulevards) and Capitole (for Place du Capitole and Rue Alsace Lorraine). The network is open from 5.15am to midnight (0.42am on Fridays and Saturdays. Trains run every 2 minutes during rush hour and every 6 minutes at other times. Car parks at several metro stations (Jolimont, Basso-Cambo, Arènes, Argoulets and Balma-Gramont) allow drivers to leave their car at the station free of charge provided they then take the metro or bus into the city (make sure you keep your used ticket until you leave the car park as you will need it to open the barrier on exit). As parking can be a problem in Toulouse and traffic is often dense, this is a much quicker and more efficient way of getting around the city centre.

Basso-Cambo — Bellefontaine — Reynerie — Mirail-Université — Bagatelle — Mermoz — Fontaine-Lestang — Arènes — Patte-d'Oie — St-Cyprien — Esquirol — Capitole — Jean-Jaurès — Marengo-SNCF — Jolimont — Roseraie — Argoulets — Balma-Gramont

LIGNE A - west/east

Borderouge — Trois Cocus — La Vache — Barière de Paris — Minimes — Canal du Midi — Compans Cafarelli — Jeanne-d'Arc — Jean-Jaurès — François Verdier — Carmes — Palais de Justice — St-Michel — St-Agne SNCF — Saouzelon — Rangueil — Fac. Pharmacie — Paul-Sabatier — Ramonville

LIGNE B - north/south

Bus network

Tickets can be bought at machines (instructions are available in English) at metro stations - be warned that many stations do not have ticket counters so you will need coins to buy tickets, though they do give change. Tickets are valid 45 minutes after validation - plenty of time for most visitors who are unlikely to travel beyond the Marengo SNCF - Jean Jaurès - Capitole-Esquirol section - and can be used on both the metro and bus networks.

Because the most interesting parts of the city are all generally accessible on foot, it is unlikely that visitors will use many of the city's 67 bus services. Apart from the airport shuttle bus, which is privately run and is detailed under the airport section, the main bus route likely to be used is route 1 which covers a circular route along the main boulevards (Lascrosses, d'Arcole, Strasbourg, Carnot). Tickets and prices are the same as for the metro. If using the bus network make sure you stamp your ticket in the machines on board.

For further details on bus services, contact **Allô Tisséo** on 05 61 41 70 70 or visit the main Tisséo office (Espace Transport) at 7, Place Esquirol. Additional information can also be obtained at the Basso-Cambo, Arènes, Marengo S.N.C.F., Jean-Jaurès and Capitole metro stations, as well as the main bus stations (*details below*) and the small bus station in Place Jeanne-d'Arc.

Bus and coach services further afield all depart from the main bus terminal (*Gare Routière des Voyageurs*) at 68, boulevard Pierre-Sémard, adjacent to the main railway station. Facilities at the bus station include a café, newsagent and left luggage office. A wide range of towns and cities are served by the terminal, both in France and abroad. Further information can be obtained directly from the coach station or by calling 05 61 61 67 67.

Car Parking

Driving in Toulouse can be extremely frustrating as traffic jams are frequent, especially around the boulevards at rush hour. Parking is a big problem in the centre; the narrow streets were not built for cars and become blocked very easily. Locals have a fairly cavalier attitude to parking - it is not uncommon to see cars parked on pavements or stopped in the middle of the streets with hazard lights flashing as the owner buys his or her bread in a nearby boulangerie. Do not be tempted to adopt these habits, however, as the police are far more present than such behaviour suggests and a five-minute risk can lead to a time-consuming and expensive visit to the city's **car pound** (tel: 05 61 12 74 80).

The city centre is well-served by underground car parks; the closest to the centre are Parking Jean Jaurès (near Place Wilson), Parking St-Etienne (near the cathedral), and Parking du Capitole (under the Place du Capitole). An easier and cheaper alternative is to avoid the traffic in the centre and take the metro, leaving your car in the car parks at certain metro stations (*see Metro System section above*).

Cycling

The *Movimento* organisation rents bikes to visitors and local residents at the main bus station and at Place Capitole (opposite the tourist office) seven days a week. A variety of bikes and cycling equipment (eg helmets, paniers, child seats) can be hired for periods ranging from half a day up to nine months. Within the city, cyclists can hire a bike for just €1 for a half day from both locations (a valid passport or identity card, deposit and metro ticket are required). Further information can be found at *Movimento*'s website at www.movimento.coop.

Exchanging money

As a general guideline, banks are open between 8.45am-12.30pm and 1.30pm-4.30pm from Monday to Friday. Some banks are also open on Saturday mornings from 8.45am until noon. Outside of these hours, most have automatic cash machines with instructions in English. The main post office listed below has a foreign exchange desk with reasonable rates, while several exchange offices are also open during and outside of normal banking hours.

The Euro

In 2002, the Euro (€) replaced the French Franc as the country's currency. There are eight denominations of coin (1, 2, 5, 10, 20 and 50 cents; and 1 and 2 euros) and seven different notes (5, 10, 20, 50, 100, 200 and 500 euros).

Lost/Stolen Credit Cards

American Express	Tel: 01 47 77 72 00.
Diner's Club	Tel: 0810 314 519.
Visa	Tel: 0800 901 179.
Mastercard/Eurocard	Tel: 0800 901 179.

Newsagents

Foreign newspapers and books are readily available in
Toulouse. Most of the daily European press is normally
available after 1p.m. on the same day. Best bets for
foreign newspapers are the following:

Librairie des Arcades:16, place du Capitole.

Presse Roosevelt kiosk, located in the central pedestrian
walkway in Allées Président Roosevelt.

Le Temps de Lire, 8, rue du Poids de l'Huile.

News Press, 65, boulevard Carnot.

The newsagents at the main railway station and the
airport also sell a wide selection of foreign newspapers
and magazines.

English Press in France French News
(tel: 05 53 06 84 40; www.french-news.com)
This monthly newspaper is produced by native English-
speakers living in France and provides a wealth of
information on events taking place in the country.

English Radio Stations

BBC World Service Radio

This can generally be received on the following
short-wave frequencies in southern France, though
reception can vary:

Channel 5 (6195) 0600 to 0930 and 1900 to 0030 GMT.

Channel 7 (9410) 0600 to 0030 GMT.

Channel 8 (12095) 0800 to 0030 GMT.

Channel 10 (15070) 1000 to 2200 GMT.

Mail

In order to make a phone call from a public telephone
you will almost certainly require *une télécarte* - a
phonecard, available from newsagents (*tabacs*) and post
offices. Ask for *une télécarte à quarante* (40) *unités/
cent vingt* (120) unités, or more simply une *petite/grande
télécarte*. Instructions in most phone booths are now
available in English. The international access code
from France is '00'. A list of country codes can be
found below. Calls within Europe are cheaper between
9.30p.m and 8a.m Monday to Friday, after 2pm
on Saturdays, and all day on Sundays. Peak rates calls
to North America are from 2pm to 8pm Mondays
to Saturdays, with reduced rates at other times.

The international code for calls made to France from
overseas is '33', though the first '0' in the ten-digit
number should not be dialled.

Stamps can be bought from post offices or from *tabacs*
(newsagents with a distinctive red cigar-shaped sign
outside). Postage rates for a postcard/letter sent from
France are as follows (max weight: 20g):
Europe: €0.54. / Worldwide: €0.90.

Main Post Office (*La Poste*)
9, rue Lafayette (located directly opposite the
Tourist Office).

Internet

Cyber Média-Net : 19, rue des Lois (tel: 05 61 23 71 45)
Net Impression : 21, avenue Billières (tel: 05 62 48 03 17)
Accès internet : 30, rue Pharaon (tel: 05 61 14 02 26).

Direct-dial country codes

The number in bold is the international access code
for each country. Figures in italics are the numbers
to be dialled to make a reverse-charge call or to use
an international calling card. This number puts you
in immediate contact with an operator in the country
dialled.

Country	Code	Country	Code
Australia:	0061	**Netherlands:**	0031
Austria:	0043	**New Zealand:**	0064
Bahrain:	00973	**Norway:**	0047
Belgium:	0032	**Portugal:**	00351
Canada:	001	**Russia:**	007
Canada Direct		**Saudi Arabia:**	00966
	0800 99 00 16	**Singapore:**	0065
China:	0086	**South Africa:**	0027
Denmark:	0045	**Spain:**	0034
Finland:	00358	**Sweden:**	0046
Germany:	0049	**Switzerland:**	0041
Greece:	0030	**Taiwan:**	00886
Hong Kong:	00852	**United Kingdom:**	0044
India:	0091	**United Arab Emirates:**	
Ireland:	00353		00971
Israel:	00972		
Italy:	0039	**United States:**	001
Japan:	0081	*0 800 99 0011* ATT	
Korea:	0082	*0 800 99 0019* MCI	
Kuwait:	00965	*0 800 99 0087* Sprint	

Toulouse has over a hundred hotels covering a wide
range of comfort and price. The following list provides a
sample of over forty hotels in and around the city which
should satisfy the requirements of all visitors. Many
hotels participate in the "*Toulouse en liberté*" scheme
offering discounts on accommodation, museums,
restaurants, tours etc. Cards (valid one year) can be
purchased from the tourist office or participating hotels;
two cards are available, one including accommodation
(adults: €13; children: €7), the other excluding
accommodation (adults: €10; children: €5). For further
information, log onto www.toulouse-tourisme.com.
Bookings can also be made via the www.reserv-hotels.fr
website or by calling 0892 700 297 (€0.34 per minute
from within France).

HOTELS - CENTRAL TOULOUSE/31000

☆☆☆☆

Sofitel Centre
84, allées Jean Jaurès.
Tel: 05 61 10 23 10 - Fax: 05 61 10 23 20.
H1091@accor.com; www.sofitel.com

Grand Hôtel de l'Opéra
1, place du Capitole. Tel: 05 61 21 82 66.
contact@grand-hotel-opera.com;
www.grand-hotel-opera.com

Crowne Plaza
7, place du Capitole. Tel: 05 61 61 19 19.
hicptoulouse@alliance-hospitality.com;
www.crowne-plaza-toulouse.com

Hôtel Garonne
22, descente de la Halle aux Poissons.
Tel: 05 34 31 94 80. contact@hotelgaronne.com;
www.hotelsdecharmetoulouse.com

☆☆☆
Hôtel Mercure Saint-Georges
Rue St-Jérôme. Tel: 05 62 27 79 79.
H0370@accor.com; www.mercure.com

Holiday Inn Toulouse Centre
15, place Wilson. Tel: 05 61 10 70 70.
hicapoul@guichard.fr; www.hotel-capoul.com

Hôtel Mercure Wilson
7, rue Labéda. Tel: 05 34 45 40 60.
H1260@accor.com; www.mercure.com

Grand Hôtel Raymond IV
16, rue Raymond IV. Tel: 05 61 62 89 41.
hotel.raymond4@wanadoo.fr;
www.hotelraymond4-toulouse.com.

Best Western Grand Hôtel Les Capitouls
29, allées Jean Jaurès.Tel: 05 34 41 31 21.
reservation@hotel-capitouls.com;
www.bestwestern-capitouls.com

Novotel Toulouse Centre
5, place Alfonse-Jourdain. Tel: 05 61 21 74 74.
H0906@accor.com; www.novotel.com

Hôtel des Beaux-Arts
1, place du Pont-Neuf. Tel: 05 34 45 42 42.
contact@hoteldesbeauxarts.com;
www.hoteldesbeauxarts.com

Hôtel Mercure Atria
8, Esplanade Compans-Caffarelli.
Tel: 05 61 11 09 09.
H1585@accor.com; www.mercure.com

Best Western Athénée
13 bis, rue Matabiau. Tel: 05 61 63 10 63.
hotel-athenee@wanadoo.fr; www.athenee-hotel.com

Hôtel de Brienne
20, boulevard Maréchal Leclerc. Tel: 05 61 23 60 60.
hoteldebrienne@wanadoo.fr; www.hoteldebrienne.com

Hôtel Mercure Matabiau
62, boulevard Pierre Semard. Tel: 05 34 41 36 70.
H1259@accor.com; www.mercure.com

Hotel Mermoz
50, rue Matabiau. Tel: 05 61 63 04 04.
reservation@hotel-mermoz.com; www.hotel-mermoz.com

☆☆

Hôtel Wilson Square
12, rue d'Austerlitz. Tel: 05 61 21 67 57.
contact@hotel-wilson.com; www.hotel-wilson.com

Hôtel Ibis Centre
2, rue Claire-Pauilhac. Tel: 05 61 63 61 63.
H1429@accor.com; www.ibishotel.com

Hôtel Castellane
17, rue Castellane. Tel: 05 61 62 18 82.
castellanehotel@wanadoo.fr; www.castellanehotel.com

Hôtel Albert Ier
8, rue Rivals. Tel: 05 61 21 17 91.
toulouse@hotel-albert1.com; www.hotel-albert.com

Hôtel Saint-Sernin
2, rue Saint Bernard.
Tel: 05 61 21 73 08 - Fax: 05 61 22 49 61.

Hôtel Royal Wilson
6, rue Labéda. Tel: 05 61 12 41 41.
www.royal-wilson.com

Hôtel Saint Claire
29, Place Bachelier. Tel: 05 34 405 888.
www.stclairehotel.fr

☆

Hôtel Croix Baragnon
17, rue Croix Baragnon. Tel: 05 61 52 60 10.
croixbaragnon@msn.com

APARTMENT HOTELS
☆☆☆

Apart'Hotel Citadines
8, boulevard de Strasbourg. Tel: 05 34 41 75 00.
wilson@citadines.com; www.citadines.com

Appart-Valley
7, rue du Pont Montaudran. Tel: 05 34 41 76 50.
toulouse@appartvalley.com; www.appartvalley.com

Parthenon
86, allées Jean Jaurès. Tel: 05 61 10 24 00.
H1910@accor.com; www.parthenon-toulouse.fr

HOTELS - OUTSKIRTS OF TOULOUSE
☆☆☆☆

Hôtel Palladia (*north-west of city*)
271, avenue de Grande-Bretagne, 31300 Toulouse.
Tel: 05 62 12 01 20.
info@hotelpalladia.com; www.hotelpalladia.com

Holiday Inn (*Toulouse Airport*)
Place de la Révolution,
31700 Blagnac
Tel: 05 34 36 00 20.
TLSAP@ichotelsgroup.com
www.toulouseairport.holiday-inn.com

☆☆☆
Airport Hôtel (*northwest of city*)
176, route de Bayonne, 31300 Toulouse.
Tel: 05 61 49 68 78. airporthotel@wanadoo.fr;
www.airport-hotel-toulouse.com

Novotel Toulouse Aéroport
23, Impasse de Maubec, 31300 Toulouse.
Tel: 05 61 15 00 00.
H0445@accor-hotels.com; www.novotel.com

☆☆
Hôtel Ibis Aéroport (*northwest of city*)
80, avenue du Parc, 31700 Blagnac.
Tel: 05 34 55 04 55.
H0798@accor.com; www.ibishotel.com

Hôtel Kyriad (*Zone Aéroportuaire Nord*)
Rue R. Grimaud, 31700 Blagnac.
Tel: 05 61 71 41 71. www.kyriad.fr

Hôtel Hermès (*north of city*)
49, avenue Jean Zay, 31200 Toulouse.
Tel: 05 61 47 60 47.
reception@hotel-hermes.com; www.hotel-hermes.com

Parc des Expositions de Toulouse
Rond-Point Michel Benech, 31000.
Tel: 05 62 25 45 45.

Centre Congrès Pierre Baudis
11, Esplanade Compans-Caffarelli, 31000.
Tel: 05 62 30 40 40; www.centre-congres-toulouse.fr.

Espace de Congrès et d'Exposition Diagora
Rue Pierre-Gilles de Gennes, 31319 Labège Cedex.
Tel: 05 61 39 93 39; www.diagora-congres.com

Restaurants

Like most major cities, Toulouse has a huge choice of
restaurants to suit every taste and budget. Although our
selection below is far from exhaustive, it covers a wide
range of options from haute cuisine to fast food, with
recommendations for sampling local as well as
international specialities.

Around Place du Capitole (parking Capitole)

Les Jardins de l'Opéra
Hôtel de l'Opéra, place du Capitole.
Tel: 05 61 23 07 76.
Closed Sunday and Monday lunchtime in summer.

Le Grand Café de l'Opéra
1, place du Capitole. Tel: 05 61 21 37 03. *Open daily.*

Le Café des Arcades
14, place du Capitole. Tel: 05 34 44 15 20. *Open daily.*

Les Caves de la Maréchale
3, rue Jules Chalande. Tel: 05 61 23 89 88. *Closed
Saturday and Monday lunchtimes and all day Sunday.*

132

La Corde
4, rue Jules Chalande. Tel: 05 61 29 09 43.
Closed Saturday lunchtimes, Sundays and Monday lunchtimes.

L'adresse
4, rue Baronie. Tel: 05 61 22 55 48.
Closed Sundays and Mondays.

La Table ronde
59, rue Pargaminières. Tel: 05 61 22 70 70. *Open daily.*

La Cave au cassoulet
54 rue Peyrolières. Tel: 05 61 13 60 30.
Closed Wednesday and Thursday lunchtimes.

La Réserve
8, rue Jean Suau. Tel: 05 61 21 84 00.
Closed Sunday and Monday.

Around Place Esquirol (parking Esquirol)

Le 19
19, Descente de la Halle aux Poissons.
Tel: 05 34 31 94 84.
Closed Saturday lunchtimes and Sundays.

Brasserie des Beaux-Arts / Chez Flo
1, quai de la Daurade. Tel: 05 61 21 12 12. *Open daily.*

La Cendrée
11-15 rue des Tourneurs. Tel: 05 61 25 76 97.
Closed Saturday lunchtimes and Sunday.

Around Place Wilson (parking Capitole)

Brasserie Le Capoul
13 Place Wilson. Tel: 05 61 21 08 27. *Open daily.*

Around Place Victor-Hugo (parking Victor-Hugo)

Marché Victor Hugo
First floor of the market building. A selection
of informal restaurants serving reasonably-priced
menus and *plats du jour*. Convivial atmosphere.
Open every lunchtime except Monday.

Le Louchebem
Marché Victor Hugo (3-4-5). Tel: 05 61 12 12 52.
Open every lunchtime except Monday.

Bistrot J'Go
16, place Victor Hugo. Tel: 05 61 23 02 03.
Closed Sundays.

La Gourmandine
15-17, place Victor-Hugo. Tel: 05 61 22 78 84.
Closed Sundays and Mondays.

Around Place Jeanne d'Arc (parking Jeanne d'Arc)

Michel, Marcel, Pierre et les Autres
35, rue de Rémusat. Tel: 05 61 22 47 05.
Closed Sundays and Mondays.

Around Gare Matabiau (parking Jeanne d'Arc)

Le Colombier
14 rue Bayard. Tel: 05 61 62 40 05
Closed Saturday lunchtimes and Sundays.

Around Place St-Georges (parking Place Occitane)

Chez Emile
13 Place St-Georges. Tel: 05 61 21 05 56
Closed Sundays and Mondays from October to April.

Restaurant du Théâtre
3 rue Labeda. Tel: 05 34 45 05 45.
Closed Sundays and Mondays.

Around Place St-Sernin (parking Arnaud Bernard)

Le 7 Place St-Sernin
7 Place St-Sernin. Tel: 05 62 30 05 30.
Closed Saturday lunchtimes and Sundays.

Around Place St-Aubin (parking St-Aubin)

Le Bouchon Lyonnais
13 rue de l'Industrie. Tel: 05 61 62 97 43.
Closed Saturday lunchtimes and Sundays.

Chez Ferdinand
14, rue de l'Etoile. Tel : 05 61 63 05 19.
Closed Sundays.

La Madeleine de Proust
11, rue Riquet. Tel: 05 61 63 80 88.
Closed Saturday lunchtimes, Sundays and Mondays.

Le Bistrot de l'Etoile
6, rue de l'Etoile. Tel: 05 61 6313 43.
Closed Saturdays and Sundays.

Around Place Dupuy (parking St-Aubin)

Le Bistrot de la Criée
42, Port St Etienne. Tel: 05 61 54 41 08.
Closed Sundays and Mondays.

Around Place des Carmes (parking des Carmes)

Rôtisserie des Carmes
38, rue des Polinaires. Tel : 05 61 53 34 88.
Closed Saturdays and Sundays.

Le Poil du Hérisson
2 rue Joutx Aigues. Tel: 05 61 53 65 23.
Closed lunchtimes and Sundays and Mondays.

La Cantine du curé
2, rue des Couteliers. Tel: 05 61 25 83 42.
Closed Sundays and Mondays.

Around Place du Parlement (parking des Carmes)
Le Petit Bacchus
16, rue Pharaon. Tel: 05 62 26 54 87. *Closed Sundays.*

31300

Le Cantou
98 rue Velasquez, Saint-Martin-du-Touch.
Tel: 05 61 49 20 21. *Closed Sundays and Mondays.*

Le Poids Gourmand
3 rue Emile Heybrard. Tel: 05 34 36 42 00.
Closed Saturday evenings, Sundays, Monday lunchtimes.

Guili Guili
230 avenue de Grande Bretagne. Tel: 05 62 12 90 97.
Closed Sundays, Mondays and Tuesdays.
Evenings only.

31400

Le Pic Saint Loup
7, rue Saint-Léon. Tel: 05 61 53 81 51.
Closed Sundays and Mondays.

Toc-Toque
35, rue des Trente-Six-Ponts.
Tel: 05 61 33 08 09. *Closed Sundays and Mondays.*

OUTSKIRTS OF TOULOUSE

31700 Blagnac

Le Bistrot Gourmand
1, bd Firmin Pons. Tel: 05 61 71 96 95.
Closed Saturday lunchtimes, Sundays and Mondays.

Restaurant du Cercle d'Oc
6 pl Marcel Dassault.
Tel: 05 62 74 71 71. *Closed Sundays and Mondays.*

Le Grand Noble
90 avenue de Cornebarrieu. Tel: 05 34 60 47 47.
Closed Friday evenings, Saturdays and Sundays.

31770 Colomiers

L'Amphytrion
Chemin de Gramont. Tel: 05 61 15 55 55. *Open daily.*

Le Canard sur le toit
58 route de la Salvetat.
Tel: 05 61 30 37 83. *Closed Sunday evenings.*

31170 Tournefeuille

L'Art de vivre
279, chemin du Ramelet Moundi. Tel: 05 61 07 52 52.
Closed Wednesday lunchtimes, Thursday, Friday
and Saturday evenings.

31130 Balma
Mas Rouge
22 route de Castres. Tel : 05 61 54 56 38.
Closed Sunday evenings.

L'Envol
Aérodrome Lasbordes. Tel: 05 61 24 59 08.
Closed Sunday, Monday, Wednesday evenings.

GLOSSARY

Viandes	Meat
Agneau	Lamb
Andouillette	Small sausage made from chitterlings
Bavette	Undercut of beef
Boeuf	Beef
Canard	Duck
Cassoulet	Local stew (see page 96)
Cervelles	Brains
Chevreuil	Venison
Confit de canard	Duck cooked and preserved in its own fat
Faux-filet	Sirloin steak
Foie	Liver
Foie gras	Fatted duck or goose liver
Gésiers	Gizzards
Jambon blanc	Cooked ham
Jambon de pays	Cured ham
Lapin	Rabbit
Lièvre	Hare
Magret de canard	Breast of duck
Manchons de canard	Duck wings
Merguez	Spicy sausage
Oie	Goose
Onglet	Prime cut of beef
Porc	Pork
Ris de veau	Calf's sweetbread
Rognons	Kidneys
Saucisse (de Toulouse)	(Toulouse) sausage
Veau	Veal
Steack	Steak can be grilled:
bleu	Very rare
saignant	Rare
à point	Medium
bien cuit	Well done

Poisson	Fish
Bar	Sea bass
Brochet	Pike
Cabillaud	Cod
Coquilles Saint Jacques	Scallops
Crevettes	Prawns
Dorade	Sea bream
Ecrevisses	Crayfish
Espadon	Swordfish
Homard	Lobster
Huitres	Oysters
Langoustines	Dublin bay prawns
Lotte	Monkfish
Loup	Bass
Moules	Mussels
Rouget	Red mullet
Sandre	Pikeperch
Saumon	Salmon
Thon	Tuna
Truite	Trout

Légumes	Vegetables
Ail	Garlic
Betterave	Beetroot
Carottes	Carrots
Chou-fleur	Cauliflower
Chou rouge	Red cabbage
Concombre	Cucumber
Cornichons	Gherkins

Epinards	Spinach
Haricots blancs	White beans
Haricots verts	Green beans
Laitue	Lettuce
Maïs	Sweetcorn
Oignon	Onion
Petits pois	Peas
Poivron vert	Green pepper
Poivron rouge	Red pepper
Pomme de terre	Potato
Radis	Radish
Salade verte	Green salad
Tomate	Tomato

Useful words

Une table non-fumeur/fumeur	A non-smoking/smoking table
La carte	The menu
La carte des vins	Wine list
Le plat du jour	Daily special
Une serviette	Napkin
Une fourchette	Fork
Un couteau	Knife
Une cuillère	Spoon
Une petite cuillère	Teaspoon
Un verre	Glass
Du sel	Salt
Du poivre	Pepper
Du sucre	Sugar
De la moutarde	Mustard
L'addition	The bill/check

Boissons / Drinks

Un café	Small expresso coffee
Un petit/grand crème	Small/large white coffee
Un déca	Decaffeinated coffee
Un thé au lait/citron	Tea with milk/lemon
Un thé déca	Decaffeinated tea
Une infusion	Herbal tea
Du lait froid/chaud	Cold/hot milk
De l'eau chaude	Hot water
Un chocolat chaud	Hot chocolate
Une carafe d'eau	Carafe of water
Un apéritif	Aperitif
Un kir	White wine with crème de cassis (blackcurrant liqueur)
Un kir royal	Champagne with crème de cassis
Un muscat	Fortified sweet white wine
Un pastis	Aniseed-flavoured aperitif (mixed with water)
Une bouteille /demi-bouteille de vin blanc/rosé/rouge	A bottle /half-bottle of white/rosé/red wine
Un verre de vin rouge /rosé/blanc	A glass of red /rosé/white wine
Un quart de vin rouge /rosé/blanc	A quarter litre carafe of red /rosé/white wine (about 2 glasses)
Une demi-carafe	A half-litre carafe
Un demi/Une pression	A glass of draught beer
Un panaché	A glass of shandy
Un digestif	Liqueur
Un armagnac	Armagnac
Une eau-de-vie	Brandy/eau-de-vie

31780 Castelginest
Le Jardin des Chimères
12 rue Pont Fauré. Tel: 05 61 70 96 44.
Closed Sundays and Mondays.

31180 *Rouffiac-Tolosan*
Ô Saveurs
8, place des Ormeaux. Tel: 05 34 27 10 11.
Closed Saturday lunchtimes, Sunday evenings and Mondays.

31520 Ramonville St-Agne
Les Marins d'Eau Douce
Parc techno du canal, place du Canal.
Tel: 05 61 73 16 15. *Closed Sundays and Mondays.*

31540 *St-Félix-Lauragais*
Auberge du Poids Public
Tel: 05 62 18 85 00. *Closed Sunday evenings.*

In the Gers department
Au Canard Gourmand
La Rente, 32130 Samatan. Tel: 05 62 62 49 81.
Closed Monday evenings and Tuesdays.

In the Aude department
Hostellerie Etienne
RN 113, 11920 Labastide-d'Anjou.
Tel: 04 68 60 10 08.
Closed Sunday and Monday evenings.

WORLD CUISINE

North /South American
Carson City
3, place Olivier, 31300. Tel: 05 61 42 02 22. *Open daily.*

El Dorado
10, descente de la Halle aux poissons, 31000.
Tel : 05 61 32 97 00. *Closed Sundays and Mondays.*

Le Seleçao
2 rue des Gestes, 31000.
Tel: 05 61 29 02 46. *Closed Sunday lunchtimes.*

Cuban
Le Puerto Habana
12 port St Etienne, 31500.
Tel: 05 61 54 45 61. *Closed Sundays.*

Italian
Cosi fan tutte
8, rue Mage, 31000. Tel: 05 62 53 07 24.
Closed Sundays and Mondays.

Il Rigoletto
2, rue Catellane, 31000. Tel: 05 61 63 19 38. *Open daily.*

La Pastasciutta
35 bis, rue Gabriel Péri, 31000. Tel: 05 61 62 69 39.

Piazzapapa
28, bd. de Strasbourg, 31000. Tel: 05 61 63 63 90. *Open daily.*
138

Pizzeria Vecchio
22, allées Jean-Jaurès, 31000. Tel: 05 62 73 34 73.
Open daily.

Scandinavian

Tante Margit
3, rue Perchepinte, 31000. Tel: 05 61 55 01 25.
Closed Saturdays and Sundays. Lunchtime only.

Spanish/Basque/Tex-Mex

Don Huevon
23, avenue du Cimetière, 31500.
Tel: 05 61 34 12 34.
Closed Saturday lunchtimes, Sundays and Mondays.

La Mesa de Lola
23, rue Compans, 31500.
Tel: 05 61 26 03 04. *Closed Sundays and Mondays.*

Mas y Mas
10, rue des Filatiers, 31000.Tel: 05 61 25 97 97.
Closed Sundays and Mondays.

El Borriquito Loco
25, rue des Paradoux, 31000. Tel: 05 61 25 34 54.
Open daily.

Bodega-Bodega
1, rue Gabriel Péri, 31000. Tel: 05 61 63 03 63.
Open daily.

Texas Café
26, rue Castellane, 31000. Tel: 05 61 99 14 15.
Open daily.

Indian

Le Bombay
11, rue des Gestes, 31000. Tel: 05 61 23 06 90.
Open daily.

Le Taj
48, rue Peyrolières, 31000. Tel: 05 61 21 84 44.
Open daily.

Le Taj Mahal
24, rue Palaprat, 31000. Tel: 05 61 99 26 80. *Open daily.*

Madras Café
67, bd de Strasbourg, 31000. Tel : 05 61 22 77 03.
Open daily.

Chinese/Japanese/Thai

La Jonque du Yang Tsé
Canal du Midi - Boulevard Griffoul-Dorval (face n°26).
Tel: 05 61 20 74 74. *Closed Mondays.*

Vietnamese

L'Empereur de Hué
17 rue Couteliers, 31000. Tel: 05 61 53 55 72.
For dinner only.

Chez Moi
28 Port Saint Sauveur, 31000. Tel: 05 61 34 29 29.
Closed Sundays.

Thai
Baan Siam
12, rue Maletache, 31000. Tel: 05 62 26 53 03.
Closed Sundays

Japanese
Le Japan
8, rue de l'Echarpe, 31000. Tel: 05 61 22 85 85.
*Closed Saturdays and Monday lunchtimes and all day
Sunday.*

North African
Dar Diaf
10, rue Maletache, 31000. Tel: 05 61 53 57 69.
Closed Sundays.

Le Marocain
47 rue des Couteliers, 31000.
Tel: 05 61 53 28 01. *Closed Monday lunchtimes.*

Le Riad
4, rue de l'Esquile, 31000. Tel: 05 34 44 91 91.
Closed Sundays.

L'Alhambra
58, rue Riquet, 31000. Tel: 05 61 62 56 49.
Closed Monday lunchtimes.

Les Deux Pachas
52, avenue Honoré Serres, 31000.
Tel: 05 61 63 99 28. *Closed Sundays.*

African
Le Mayombé
26, rue de la République, 31300. Tel: 05 61 59 50 50.
Open daily.

Vegetarian/Organic Restaurants
Saveur Bio
22, rue Maurice-Fonvieille, 31000. Tel : 05 61 12 15 15.
Closed Sundays.

Le Bol Bu
8, rue du May, 31000. Tel: 05 61 21 11 31.
Closed Sundays.

Scop Bioasis
21, rue des Amidonniers, 31000. Tel: 05 61 13 99 67.
Closed Sundays.

Pubs/Cafés/ Tea Rooms

London Town 14, rue des Prêtres, 31000.
Tel: 05 61 53 36 98. *Open daily.*

Killarney Pub
14, rue Alfred Dumeril, 31000. Tel: 05 62 26 52 04.
Open daily.

The Frog & Rosbif
14, rue de l'Industrie, 31000. Tel: 05 61 99 28 57.
Open daily.

Le Dubliners
46, avenue Marcel Langer, 31400. Tel: 05 61 14 23 16.
Closed Sundays.

Hoegaarden Café
52, route de Narbonne, 31400. Tel: 0 825 280 120.
Open daily.

The Bell
Centre Commercial Sainte-Germaine, 31820 Pibrac
(5 km west of airport). Tel: 05 61 86 01 74.
Closed Sundays.

Le Petit London
7 bis, rue Riquet, 31000. Tel: 05 61 62 93 29.

La Maison
9 rue Gabriel Péri, 31000 Toulouse. Tel: 05 61 62 87 22.

Maximo café
3, rue Gabriel Péri, 31000. Tel: 05 61 62 08 07.
Le Breughel
30, rue de la Chaîne, 31000. Tel: 05 61 21 66 54.

Bistrot Voyageur
14, place Arnaud-Bernard, 31000. Tel: 05 61 23 90 78.

Le Cube
5, rue Pargaminières, 31000. Tel: 05 61 21 89 08.

Bar Tchin Tchin
22, rue St-Bernard, 31000. Tel: 05 61 21 35 08.

Le Caribe Café
12, Place Victor Hugo, 31000. Tel: 05 61 22 45 99.

Le Seventies
42, Port St-Etienne, 31000. Tel: 05 61 80 72 17.

Les Avions
3, place des Avions, 31400. Tel: 05 61 52 90 70.

Entertainment

Le Bijou
123, avenue de Muret, 31300. Tel: 05 61 42 95 07.

A bord du Chèvrefeuille
Péniche Chevrefeuille, av. Sables
31520 Ramonville-St-Agne.
Tel: 05 61 73 39 31/ 05 62 19 08 08.

Havana Café
2, Boulevard des Crêtes, 31520
Ramonville St-Agne. Tel: 05 62 88 34 94.

Tea rooms

Saveur des Tropiques
5, place Rouaix, 31000. Tel: 05 61 25 26 75.

L'instant Thé
34, rue de la Colombette, 31000. Tel : 05 61 62 04 35

Gusto Café
7, rue Temponières, 31000. Tel: 05 62 30 91 90.

Dip's tea
28, rue Pharaon, 31000. Tel: 05 61 32 68 16.

Le Cosy Caffé
10, Place Stes-Scarbes, 31000. Tel: 05 612 26 35 25.

Interlude Café
14, 15 Place Jeanne-D'Arc, 31000. Tel: 05 61 62 43 56.

Ice cream
La Boutique des Saveurs
1, rue Ozenne, 31000. Tel: 05 61 53 75 21

Au Cornet d'amour
28, rue Montardy, 31000. Tel: 05 62 27 13 40.

For non-European Union visitors, VAT refunds are available on minimum purchases of €183 made in the same shop. To benefit from this, ask for a tax refund form (*bordereau de détaxe*) which should be presented to Customs (*La Douane*) on leaving the country.

Regional Specialities

Bacquié
5, place Victor Hugo. Tel: 05 61 23 39 87.

Samaran
18, place Victor Hugo. Tel: 05 61 21 26 91.

Cheeses

Sena Fromager
Marché des Carmes, loge 51. Tel: 05 61 14 24 61.

Betty
Marché Victor Hugo. Tel: 05 61 22 17 81.

Wines & Spirits

Busquets
21, place Victor Hugo. Tel: 05 61 21 46 22.

Domaine de Lastours
44, rue du Languedoc. Tel: 05 61 52 05 20.

Chocolates

Au Poussin bleu
45, rue du Languedoc. Tel: 05 61 52 01 70.

Yves Thuriès
69, rue d'Alsace-Lorraine. Tel: 05 61 12 07 79.

Atelier du chocolat de Bayonne
1, rue du Rempart-Villeneuve. Tel: 05 61 22 97 67.

Wholefood Shops

Le Moulin
40, rue Peyrolières. Tel: 05 61 21 71 97.

Grandeur nature
19, avenue des Ecoles-Jules-Julien, 31400.
Tel: 05 61 53 95 63.

Markets

Place Victor Hugo
Open Tuesday to Sunday until 1pm. The largest indoor market in the city. Numerous stalls selling fruit and vegetables, fish, meat and cheeses. The first floor is a Toulouse lunchtime institution.

Place St-Aubin
Sunday mornings. A delightful market with a rural character. Stalls selling fruits, vegetables, meat, cheeses, live poultry and other small animals.

Place des Carmes
Open Tuesday to Sunday. Smaller indoor market than Place Victor Hugo but excellent quality nonetheless. Good view of the city from the top floor of the car park above it.

Boulevard de Strasbourg
Tuesday to Sunday mornings, closed Monday. Huge fruit and vegetable market. Several attractive flower stalls.

Place St-Georges
Tuesday to Saturday mornings. Small fruit, vegetable and flower market.

Place Saint-Sernin
Sunday mornings. Large flea market around Saint-Sernin basilica.

Place du Capitole
Tuesdays and Saturdays. Small fruit and vegetable market, plus an organic section. The Wednesday all-day market sells a range of clothes, books and fashion accessories.

Golf Clubs

Golf Club de Vieille-Toulouse
31320 Vieille Toulouse (*a couple of kilometres south of the city*). Tel: 05 61 73 45 48. 18-hole course on a hill overlooking the Garonne river and Toulouse - Par 70. Club hire possible. Restaurant. *Open daily.*

Golf Club de Palmola
31660 Buzet-sur-Tarn (*20 kilometres north-east*). Tel: 05 61 84 20 50. 18 holes - Par 72. Pool, restaurant. Open to non-members. No club hire. *Closed Tuesday.*

Golf de la Ramée
Ferme du Cousturier, 31170 Tournefeuille (*15 minutes from the city centre*). Tel: 05 61 07 09 09. *Open daily.* Two courses: an 18-hole par 70 and 9-hole pitch and putt.

Tennis

Tennis des Argoulets
Chemin de Rabastens, 31500 Toulouse. Tel: 05 61 26 34 20. 6 outdoor/3 indoor courts.

Tennis des Ponts-Jumeaux
Rue des Sports, 31200 Toulouse. Tel: 05 61 57 17 39. 3 outdoor (including 1 floodlit) and 3 indoor courts.

Squash

Espace Biotonic, 98 bis, chemin de la Flambère, 31300.
Tel: 05 61 49 30 79. Five courts. *Open daily.*

Aérosquash de Blagnac
94, route de Cornebarrieu, 31700 Blagnac.
Tel: 05 61 71 94 07. Six courts. *Open daily.*

Swimming Pools

Espace Nautique Jeau Vauchère
Place des fêtes, 31770 Colomiers.
Tel: 05 34 60 43 43. *Open all year.*

Léo Lagrange
Place Riquet, 31000. Tel: 05 61 22 24 15.
Olympic-sized indoor pool.
Closed from 1 July to mid-September.

Alfred Nakache/Parc des Sports
Allées Gabriel-Biénès.
Tel: 05 61 22 31 35 or 05 61 22 30 14.
Two outdoor pools, one the biggest in Europe
(150m long). *Open all year.*

Ice-Skating

Patinoire Jacques Raynaud
10, avenue du Général De Gaulle, 31700, Blagnac.
Tel: 05 62 74 71 40.
This 60m x 30m rink is open daily. Skate hire available.

Horse Racing

Hippodrome La Cépière
1, chemin des Courses (avenue de Lombez),
31100. Tel: 05 61 49 27 24.
www.hippodrome-toulouse.com.
Flat racing, steeplechasing and trotting meetings. *All year
except July and August.* Evening trotting meetings on
Thursday and Friday during the summer months.

Yoga

Association Yoga Midi-Pyrénées
9 allées du Breuil, 31320 Vigoulet-Auzil.
Tel: 05 61 73 28 58. The region's governing body for
yoga offers lessons and courses for all levels.

L'Institut du Yoga Traditionnel de Toulouse
2, chemin de Canti, 31320 Vieille-Toulouse.
Tel: 05 61 75 69 15.
Lessons for beginners and advanced yoga students.

Tai Chi

Centre Sportif Léo Lagrange
54, rue des Troubadours, 31000. Tel: 05 61 62 80 30.

Aikido

Dojo de la Roseraie
4, chemin Nicol, 31500. Tel: 05 61 26 10 31.
Daily lunchtime and evening classes.

Keiko
Karate
6bis, rue Champêtre.Tel: 05 61 42 12 02.
Karate, kendo and tai chi classes for adults and children.

Judo Toulouse
Judo
26, route d'Albi, Croix Daurade, 31200.
Tel: 05 61 48 03 48. Classes for participants aged 5
and upwards.

Roman Catholic
Cathédrale Saint-Etienne, place St-Etienne.
Tel: 05 61 52 03 82.
S*ervices in French*: Saturday at 6.30p.m
Sunday at 9.30 and 11a.m
Basilique St-Sernin, place St-Sernin. Tel: 05 61 21 80 45.
Services in French: Sunday at 9.00, 10.30a.m and 6.30p.m.

Protestant
Temple du Salin, place du Salin, 4, impasse de la
Trésorie; 31000. Tel: 05 61 52 73 93.
Ser*vices in French*: Sunday at 10.30a.m.

Anglican
Sainte-Marguerite, 105, avenue des Arènes-Romaines,
31300. Tel: 05 61 85 17 67.
Services in English: Sunday at 10.30a.m.

Orthodox
Saint Nicolas: 302, avenue de Grande Bretagne, 31300.
Tel: 05 61 31 92 25.
Services mainly in French: Saturday at 6p.m, Sunday
10a.m in summer and 10.30a.m in winter.

Jewish
Synagogue: 2, rue Palaprat, 31000.
Tel: 05 61 62 90 41.

Muslim
Mosque (*Mosquée*)
257, route de Seysses, 31100.
Tel: 05 61 44 55 65.

Buddhism
Institut Vajra Yogini (Tibetan buddhism)
81500 Marzens (*40 kms to the east of Toulouse
and 6 kms from Lavaur, in the Tarn*);
9, avenue de Lagarde, c/o La Mane, 31130 Balma.
Tel: 05 63 58 17 22. Tuesday at 8.30p.m.

Australia
Embassy: 4, rue Jean Rey, 75015 Paris.
Tel: 01 40 59 33 00; www.france.embassy.gov.au

Belgium
3, rue Mage, 31000. Tel: 05 61 52 67 93.

Canada
10, rue Jules de Resseguier, 31000.
Tel: 05 61 99 30 16;
consulat.canada.toulouse@wanadoo.fr

Denmark
41, rue Alsace-Lorraine, 31000.
Tel: 05 34 44 98 37; www.amb-danemark.fr

Finland
32, chemin Salinié, 31100.
Tel: 05 61 49 75 02; adg3@wanadoo.fr

Germany
24, rue de Metz, 31000.
Tel: 05 61 52 35 56; www.amb-allemagne.fr

Greece
Embassy: 17, rue Auguste Vacquerie, 75116 Paris.
Tel: 01 47 23 72 28; www.amb-grece.fr

Ireland
Embassy: 4, rue Rude, 75116 Paris.
Tel: 01 44 17 67 00;
www.foreignaffairs.gov.ie/irishembassy

Italy
13, rue Alsace-Lorraine, 31000. Tel: 05 34 45 48 48;
cons.tolosa@magic.fr

Japan
Embassy: 7, avenue Hoche, 75008 Paris.
Tel: 01 48 88 62 00; www.fr.emb-japan.go.jp

Netherlands
54 bis, rue Alsace Lorraine, 31000.
Tel: 05 61 13 64 94; www.amb-pays-bas.fr

New Zealand
Embassy: 7ter, rue Léonardo de Vinci, 75116 Paris.
Tel: 01 45 00 24 11; www.nzembassy.com

Norway
9, rue Matabiau, 31000.
Tel: 05 62 73 44 22.

Portugal
33, avenue Camille Pujol, 31500.
Tel: 05 61 80 43 45; www.embaixada-portugal-fr.org

South Africa
Embassy: 59, quai d'Orsay, 75343 Paris.
Tel: 01 53 59 23 23; www.afriquesud.net

Spain
16, rue Ste-Anne, 31000.
Tel: 05 34 31 96 60; www.amb-espagne.fr

Sweden
Embassy: 17, rue Barbet de Jouy, 75007 Paris.
Tel: 01 44 18 88 00; www.swedenabroad.com

Switzerland
Embassy: 142, rue Grenelle, 75007 Paris.
Tel: 01 49 55 67 00; www.amb-suisse.fr

United States
25, allées Jean-Jaurès, 31000.
Tel: 05 34 41 36 50; www.amb-usa.fr

United Kingdom
353, boulevard du president Wilson,
33073 Bordeaux.
Tel: 05 57 22 21 10; www.britishembassy.gov.uk

Germany - Goethe Institut
4 bis, rue Clémence Isaure, 31000.
Tel: 05 61 23 08 34; www.goethe.de/toulouse

Spain - Institut Cervantes
31, rue des Chalets, 31000.
Tel: 05 61 62 80 72; www.cervantes-toulouse.fr

Italy - Dante Alighieri
9, place du Capitole, 31000. Tel: 05 61 21 12 15.

China - Alliance franco-chinoise
25, rue Denfert-Rochereau, 31000.
Tel: 05 61 61 00 17; www.alliancefranco-chinoise.com

Russia - Association Toulouse CEI
38, rue Pargaminières, 31000.
Tel: 05 61 21 18 74; www.toulousecei.free.fr

Residency Information

EU citizens who are intending to reside or work in
France for a period of more than three months should
apply to the *Préfecture* for a *carte de séjour*.

Préfecture
Service des Étrangers (Foreign resident section)
1, rue St-Anne, 31000. Tel: 05 34 45 34 45.

Toulouse Accueil association
2, place des Carmes, 31000.
Tel: 05 61 55 39 81; www.avf.asso.fr
The aim of this organisation is to welcome all new
arrivals to Toulouse. *Open daily.*

French Centre for International Exchange (EGIDE)
18, place Roguet, 31300.
Tel: 05 61 77 26 66; www.egide.asso.fr

English-Speaking Associations

Toulouse Women's International Group
www.twigsite.org
A group which organises activities and provides advice
and help to locally-based English-speaking women of all
nationalities.

Americans in Toulouse
www.americansintoulouse.com
In addition to encouraging integration into French life,
the aim of A.I.T. is to organise a range of social
and cultural activities, act as a support group, foster
friendships and provide an outlet for information of
general interest to its members, who include people from
the United States and other English-speaking countries.

Association France/Etats-Unis
www.france-etatsunis.com
The aim of this association is to encourage and develop
friendly, cultural links between the United States and
France, particularly between Americans living in the
Midi Pyrénées and local people.

Le Grand Toulouse
1, place de la Légion d'Honneur, BP 35821,
31505 Toulouse cedex 5. Tel: 05 34 49 59 00.
www.grandtoulouse.org

Mairie de Toulouse (City Hall)
Place du Capitole. Tel: 05 61 22 21 43; www.toulouse.fr

Conseil Général de la Haute-Garonne
(Haute-Garonne Local Authority)
1, boulevard de la Marquette, 31000. Tel: 05 34 33 32 31;
www.haute-garonne.fr

Conseil Régional (Midi-Pyrénées Regional Authority)
22, boulevard du Maréchal Juin, 31400.
Tel: 05.61.33.50.50; www.midipyrenees.fr

Office de Tourisme (Tourist Office)
Donjon du Capitole. Tel: 05 61 11 02 22;
www.toulouse-tourisme.com. *Open daily.*

CDT Haute-Garonne (Haute-Garonne Tourist Board)
14, rue Bayard, 31000. Tel: 05 61 99 44 00;
www.cdt-haute-garonne.fr

CRT Midi-Pyrénées (Midi-Pyrénées Tourist Board)
54, boulevard de l'Embouchure, 31000.
Tel: 05 61 13 55 55; www.tourisme-midi-pyrenees.com

Tourist Offices in Midi-Pyrénées
(See Excursions, pages 98-119):

Cordes-sur-Ciel
Maison Fonpeyrouse and Place Jeanne Ramel-Cals,
81170 Cordes-sur-Ciel.
Tel: 05 63 56 00 52; www.cordes-sur-ciel.org

Albi
Palais de la Berbie, Place Ste-Cécile, 81000 Albi.
Tel: 05 63 49 48 80; www.albi-tourisme.fr

Castres
3, rue Milhau, Ducommun, 81100 Castres.
Tel: 05 63 62 63 62; www.tourisme-castres.fr

Moissac
6, place Durand de Bredon, 82200 Moissac.
Tel: 05 63 04 01 85; www.moissac.fr

Montauban
4, rue du Collège, 82000 Montauban.
Tel: 05 63 63 60 60; www.montauban-tourisme.com

Saint-Antonin-Noble-Val

23, place de la Mairie,
82140 Saint-Antonin-Noble-Val. Tel: 05 63 30 63 47;
www.saint-antonin-nobleval.com

Najac

Place du Faubourg, 12270 Najac. Tel: 05 65 29 72 05.

Villefranche-de-Rouergue

Promenade du Giraudet, 12200 Villefranche-de-Rouergue.
Tel: 05 65 45 13 18; www.villefranche.com

Auch

1, rue Dessoles, 32000 Auch.
Tel: 05 62 05 22 89; www.auch-tourisme.com

Flaran

Abbaye de Flaran, 32310 Valence-sur-Baïse.
Tel: 05 62 28 50 19; www.gers-gascogne.com

Foix

29, rue Delcassé, 09000 Foix.
Tel: 05 61 65 12 12; www.ot-foix.fr

Montségur

104 ter Village, 09300 Montségur. Tel: 05 61 03 03 03.
www.citaenet.com / www.montsegur.org

St-Bertrand-de-Comminges

Les Olivetains, Parvis de la Cathédrale,
31510 St-Bertrand-de-Comminges.
Tel: 05 61 95 44 44. olivetains.tourisme-haute-garonne.com

Carcassonne

Tourist Office: 28, rue de Verdun,
11890 Carcassonne. Tel: 04 68 10 24 30;
www.carcassonne-tourisme.com
There is also a tourist office in the Tour Narbonnaise
in the Cité.

Weather Forecasts

Météo France (French Meteorological Office):
www. meteofrance.com

Météo consult: www.meteoconsult.fr

Research Centres

Association Aéronautique et Astronautique de France
(AAAF)
Campus de l'IAS, 23, av. E. Belin, 31400 Toulouse.
Tel: 05 62 17 52 80 - Fax: 05 62 17 52 81.
www.aaaf.asso.fr

Aerospace Valley
2, av. E. Belin, B.P. 4025, 31055 Toulouse cedex 4.
Tel: 05 61 14 80 30 - Fax: 05 62 26 46 25.
wwwaerospace-valley.com

Centre National d'Etudes Spatiales (CNES)
18, avenue E. Belin, 31401 Toulouse cedex.
Tel: 05 61 27 31 31 - Fax: 05 61 27 31 79. www.cnes.fr

Centre d'Essais Aéronautiques de Toulouse (CEAT)
47, rue Saint-Jean, 31130 Balma.
Tél : 05 62 57 57 57 - Fax : 05 62 57 54 47.

Centre d'Etudes et de Recherches de Toulouse
(ONERA - CERT)
2, avenue E. Belin, B.P. 4025, 31055 Toulouse cedex 4.
Tel: 05 62 25 25 25 - Fax: 05 62 25 25 50. www.cert.fr

Laboratoire d'Automatique et d'analyse des systèmes
(LAAS)
7, avenue du Colonel Roche. 31077 Toulouse cedex 4.
Tel: 05 61 33 62 00 - Fax: 05 61 55 35 77. www.laas.fr

Institut National de la Recherche Agronomique (INRA)
Chem. de Borde-Rouge. Auzeville. B. P. 52627
31326 Castanet-Tolosan cedex.
Tel: 05 61 28 50 28 - Fax: 05 61 28 52 80. www.inra.fr

Centre National de la Recherche Scientifique (CNRS)
Délégation régionale
16, avenue E. Belin, B. P. 4367, 31054 Toulouse cedex 4.
Tel: 05 61 33 60 00 - Fax: 05 62 17 29 01.
www.cnrs.fr/midi-pyrenees

Observatoire Midi-Pyrénées
14, av. E. Belin, 31400 Toulouse.
Tel: 05 61 33 29 29 - Fax: 05 61 33 28 88.www.obs-mip.fr

Institut National des Sciences Appliquées (INSA)
135, avenue de Rangueil, 31077 Toulouse cedex 4.
Tel: 05 61 55 95 13 - Fax: 05 61 55 95 00.
www.insa-toulouse.fr

Institut National de la Santé et de la Recherche
Médicale (INSERM)
CHU de Purpan, B. P. 3048. 31024 Toulouse cedex 3.
Tel: 05 62 74 83 50 - Fax: 05 61 31 97 52.
www.toulouse.inserm.fr

Centre de Promotion de la Recherche Scientifique
(CPRS) Université de Toulouse-Le Mirail, Maison de la
Recherche, 5, allées A. Machado, 31058 Toulouse cedex 1.
Tel: 05 61 50 44 68 - Fax: 05 61 50 37 14.
www.univ-tlse2.fr

Schools / Universities

École Nationale de l'Aviation Civile (ENAC)
7, avenue E.-Belin, 31055 Toulouse cedex 4.
Tel: 05 62 17 40 00 - Fax: 05 62 17 40 23. www.enac.fr

École Nationale Supérieure de l'Aéronautique et de l'Espace (SUPAERO):
10, avenue E.-Belin, 31400 Toulouse.
Tel: 05 62 17 80 80 - Fax: 05 62 17 83 30.
www.supaero.fr

École Nationale Supérieure d'Ingénieurs de Constructions Aéronautiques (ENSICA)
1, place Emile Blouin, 31056 Toulouse cedex 5.
Tel: 05 61 61 85 00 - Fax: 05 61 61 85 85.
www.ensica.fr

Institut National Polytechnique de Toulouse
6, allées Émile Monso, B.P. 4038,
31029 Toulouse cedex 4.
Tel: 05 62 25 54 00 - Fax: 05 62 24 21 00.
www.inp-toulouse.fr

École Nationale Supérieure Électrotechnique, Électronique Informatique et Hydraulique de Toulouse (INP/ENSEEIHT)
2, rue Charles-Camichel, B.P. 122,
31071 Toulouse cedex 7.
Tel: 05 61 58 82 00 - Fax: 05 61 62 09 76.
www.enseeiht.fr

École Nationale Supérieure d'Ingénieur en Arts Chimiques et Technologiques (INP/ENSIACET)
118, route de Narbonne, 31400 Toulouse.
Tel: 05 62 88 56 56 - Fax: 05 62 08 56 00.
www.ensiacet.fr

École Nationale Supérieure Agronomique de Toulouse
(INP/ENSAT): Av. de l'Agrobiopole, B.P. 107,
31326 Castanet-Tolosan cedex.
Tel: 05 62 19 39 00 - Fax: 05 62 19 39 01. www.ensat.fr

École Nationale de Formation Agronomique (ENFA)
RN 113, 31326 Auzeville-Tolosane.
Tel: 05 61 75 32 32 - Fax: 05 61 75 03 09.
www.ensa.fr

École Supérieure d'Agriculture de Purpan (ESAP)
75, voie Toec, 31076 Toulouse cedex.
Tel: 05 61 15 30 30 - Fax: 05 61 15 30 00.
www.purpan.fr

École Nationale de Météorologie (ENM)
42, avenue Gaspard Coriolis, 31057 Toulouse cedex 1.
Tel: 05 61 07 90 90 - Fax: 05 61 07 96 30.
www.enm.meteo.fr

École Nationale Vétérinaire de Toulouse (ENVT)
23 chemin des Capelles, BP 87614, 31076 Toulouse cedex.
Tel: 05 61 19 38 00 - Fax: 05 61 19 38 18.
www.envt.fr

École Supérieure de Commerce (ESC)
BP 7010, 20, boulevard Lascrosses, 31000.
Tel: 05 61 29 49 49 - Fax: 05 61 29 49 94.
www.esc-toulouse.fr

École Nationale Supérieure d'Architecture
83, rue Aristide Maillol, 31106 Toulouse cedex 1.
Tel: 05 62 11 50 50 - Fax: 05 62 11 50 99.
www.toulouse.archi.fr

Université Paul Sabatier (Toulouse III)
118, route de Narbonne, 31062 Toulouse cedex 9.
Tel: 05 61 55 66 11 - Fax: 05 61 55 64 70.
International Relations Division: 05 61 55 66 24.
www.ups-tlse.fr

Faculté de Médecine - Rangueil (Faculty of Medecine)
133, route de Narbonne, 31062 Toulouse
Tel: 05 62 88 90 00.
www.medecine.ups-tlse.fr

Faculté de Médecine - Purpan (Faculty of Medecine)
37, allées Jules-Guesde, 31073.
Tel: 05 61 14 59 07.
www.medecine.ups-tlse.fr

Faculté des Sciences pharmaceutiques
(Faculty of Pharmacy):
35, chemin des Maraîchers, 31400.
Tel: 05 62 25 68 00. www.pharmacie.ups-tlse.fr

Faculté de Chirurgie Dentaire (dental Surgery)
3, chemin des Maraîchers, 31400.
Tel: 05 62 17 29 29.
www.dentaire.ups-tlse.fr

IUT Paul Sabatier
115, route de Narbonne, 31077 Toulouse cedex.
Tel: 05 62 25 80 00 - Fax: 05 62 25 80 01.
www.iut.tlse3.fr

Réseau Universitaire Toulouse Midi-Pyrénées
15, rue des Lois, 31000.
Tel: 05 61 14 80 10 - Fax: 05 61 14 80 20.
www.rutmp.fr

Université des Sciences Sociales (Toulouse I)
2, rue du Doyen Gabriel-Marty,
31042 Toulouse cedex 9.
Tel: 05 61 63 35 00 - Fax: 05 61 63 37 98.
www.univ-tlse1.fr
International Relations Division: 05 61 63 36 45.
Manufacture des Tabacs: 21, allées de Brienne, 31000.
Tel: 05 61 12 85 00 - Fax: 05 61 12 86 75.

Institut d'Etudes Politiques
2 ter, rue des Puits Creusés, 31685 Toulouse cedex 6.
Tel: 05 61 11 02 60. Fax: 05 61 22 94 80.
www.sciencespo-toulouse.fr
International Relations Division: 05 61 11 56 87.

Université de Toulouse le Mirail (Toulouse II)
5, allées Antonio Machado, 31058 Toulouse cedex 9.
Tel: 05 61 50 42 50 - Fax: 05 61 50 42 09.
www.univ-tlse2.fr
International Relations Division: 05 61 50 42 50.

Institut Universitaire de Formation des Maîtres
(I.U.F.M.)
56, avenue de l'URSS, 31004 Toulouse cedex 6.
Tel: 05 62 25 20 00 - Fax: 05 62 25 20 68.
www.ent.toulouse.iufm.fr

Centre Régional Éducation Populaire et de Sports
(CREPS): 1, av. E. Belin, BP 373,
31055 Toulouse cedex 4.
Tel: 05 62 17 90 00 - Fax: 05 62 17 90 01.
www.midi-pyrenees.jeunesse-sports.gouv.fr

Institut Catholique
31, rue de la Fonderie, 31000.
Tel: 05 61 36 81 00 - Fax: 05 61 55 39 28.
www.ict-toulouse.asso.fr

Lycée Polyvalent International
Boulevard Victor Hugo,
BP 313, 31773 Colomiers cedex.
Tel: 05 61 15 94 94 - Fax: 05 61 30 35 91.
www.pedagogie.ac-toulouse.fr
British section: 05 61 78 71 28 - www.english31.com
Deutsche Schule Toulouse (German high school):
Tel: 05 61 78 36 40. www.dstoulouse.cjb.net

The International School of Toulouse
2, allées de l'Herbaudière, route de Pibrac
31770 Colomiers.
Tel: 05 62 74 26 74 - Fax: 05 62 74 26 75.
www.intst.eu

Local Education Authority

Rectorat : Impasse Saint-Jacques, 31000.
Tel: 05 61 36 40 00 - Fax: 05 61 52 80 27.

**Centre Régional des Œuvres Universitaires et
Scolaires (CROUS)** : 58, rue du Taur, 31000.
Tel: 05 61 12 54 00 - Fax: 05 61 12 54 07.

154

Notes

Notes